ALBERT 7
THEOLOGIAN A.   ιST

Bibliographic Resources
and
Translated Essays

Translated and Edited by
Thomas F. O'Meara, O.P.

NEW PRIORY PRESS

EXPLORING THE DOMINICAN VISION

Introduction

A growing number of books and essays have appeared on Albert of Lauingen, "Albert the Great," in the past decade. They have gone beyond presenting his relationship to Thomas Aquinas to give a picture of a varied intellectual personality. Showing him as more than a pioneer in the examinations of natural science and an expositor of Aristotelian philosophy, these studies present not only his philosophy and science but his theology of God, the church, the human person, and the sacraments. And too, Albert is seen as a remarkable figure in European political structures, civic and ecclesiastical.

The following collection aims at offering something of the variety and breadth of Albert's intellectual life, theological efforts, and influence.

First there is a survey of past and present studies on his personality and thought; particular attention is paid to the many publications of the past twenty-five years. Second, there are translations of ten recent studies whose topics range from church authority to political conflict, from eschatology to Albert portrayed in art.

Two bibliographical resources should be mentioned at the beginning: Irven M. Resnick & Kenneth F. Kitchell, Jr., *Albert the Great: A Selectively Annotated Bibliography (1900 – 2000)* (Tempe: Arizona Center for Medieval and Renaissance Studies, 2004); Jörgen Vijgen, "Albertus Magnus – A Selective Bibliography," *Nederlands Thomas Genootschap*. Above all, there is the Institut devoted to Albert the Great in Bonn with its scholars, publications, and important website.

Thomas F. O'Meara, O.P.

August 8, 2013

Authors and Articles

Thomas F. O'Meara, O.P. "Resources and Recent Publications on Albert the Great and His Theology"

Thomas F. O'Meara, Warren Professor Emeritus, University of Notre Dame (USA) with writings on medieval and modern theologians.

Alain de Libera, "Albert the Great, 1200-1280," *Dictionnaire du Moyen Âge* (Paris: Presses Universitaires de France, 2002) 26-29.

Alain de Libera, author of studies on Pseudo-Dionysius and theologians and philosophers in the thirteenth century, and on Albert the Great and his students.

Joachim Söder, "Albert the Great, 'the Astonishing Wonder'," *Wort und Antwort* 41 (2000): 145-47.

Joachim Söder, author of studies on Dominican and Franciscan medieval theologians and member of the Albertus-Magnus-Institut (Bonn).

Cardinal Karl Lehmann, *Albert the Great's Conception of Theology. Studia Albertina* # 8 (Münster: Aschendorff, 2006).

Karl Lehmann, professor at the University of Mainz, Bishop of Mainz and Cardinal, and longtime President of the German Episcopal Conference.

Ulrich Horst, "Albertus Magnus and Thomas Aquinas as Commentators on *The Gospel according to Matthew* 16:18. A Contribution to the Teaching on Papal Primacy,"

Ulrich Horst, author of studies on medieval theologians and on the ecclesiology of the Baroque era, and former director of the Grabmann Institut at the Ludwig-Maximilians-Universität (Munich).

Hans Jorissen, *The Contribution of Albert the Great to the Theological Reception of Aristotle: The Example of Transubstantiation. Lectio Albertina* # 5 (Münster: Aschendorff, 2002).

Hans Jorissen, author of studies on medieval thought, members of the teaching faculty at the University of Bonn, and past adviser for the Critical Edition of the Works of Albert the Great appearing from the Albertus-Magnus-Institut (Bonn).

Henryk Anzulewicz, "The Priesthood and Religious Life according to Albertus Magnus, "Thomas Prügl and Marianne Schlosser, eds., *Dominikanische Beiträge zur Ekklesiologie und zum kirchlichen Leben im Mittelalter* (Paderborn: Schöningh, 2007) 63-86

Henryk Anzulewicz, "The End and Renewal of the World (Matthew 5:18; 24:35)," *Wort und Antwort* 41 (2000): 183-87.

Henryk Anzulewicz, author of many studies of Albert and member of Albertus-Magnus-Institut (Bonn).

Rudolf Schieffer, *Albertus Magnus. Mendicancy and Theology in Conflict with Episcopacy. Lectio Albertina # 3* (Münster: Aschendorff, 1999).

Rudolf Schieffer, Professor at the Ludwig-Maximilians-Universität (Munich) and since 1983 President of the Monumenta Germaniae Historica (Munich).

Hugo Stehkämper, "Albertus Magnus and the Cologne Reconciliation of April 17, 1271," *Wort und Antwort* 41 (2000): 170-73.

Hugo Stehkämper, retired professor and archivist whose publications often focus on the history of Cologne.

Erhard Schlieter, "Albert the Great in Art," *Wort und Antwort* 41 (2000): 174-79.

Erhard Schlieter, expert on the history and culture of Cologne, and on Albert the Great in that world.

Table of Contents

Thomas F. O'Meara, O.P.

Resources and Recent Publications on
Albert the Great and His Theology

Publications in recent years have suggested composing this survey of resources on the theology of Albert of Lauingen. Books and articles, monographs and collections of essays, critical texts and bibliographies have appeared and more are continuing to be published. Jan Aertsen speaks of a strong interest in Albert beginning in the 1980s. "In this 'Albert-Renaissance' two motifs are at work. The first wants to present Albert's own identity....One should not consider Albert only in relationship to Thomas or as someone standing in the shadow of his student....The second motif is to see him as *Albertus teutonicus*, the source of the German Dominican school."[1] The following essay illustrates contemporary interest in Albert, even as it joins to this some past resources for his theology.

Albert was a Swabian scholar and a Dominican friar, a pioneer of the use of Aristotelian philosophy in Western Christian theology and a natural scientist. He was the teacher of Thomas Aquinas, Ulrich of Strassburg, and perhaps of Meister Eckhart. Ulrich wrote of him: "My teacher...was an almost divine person in every science, so much so that

---

[1] Jan A. Aertsen "Albertus Magnus und die mittelalterliche Philosophie," *Allgemeine Zeitschrift für Philosophie* 21 (1996): 111-113. From the anniversary year of 1980 come Loris Sturlese, "Albert der Grosse und die deutsche philosophische Kultur des Mittelalters," *Freiburger Zeitschrift für Philosophie und Theologie* 27 (1981): 133-47 and three works by James Athanasius Weisheipl: *Albertus Magnus and the Sciences. Commemorative Essays, 1980* (Toronto: Pontifical Institute of Mediaeval Studies, 1980), *Thomas d'Aquino and Albert His Teacher* (Toronto: Pontifical Institute of Mediaeval Studies, 1980) 3-53, and "Albert the Great and Medieval Culture," *The Thomist* 44 (1980): 481-501; Gerbert Meyer and Albert Zimmerman, eds. *Albertus Magnus, Doctor Universalis, 1280/1980* (Mainz: Matthias Grünewald, 1980). There is an issue of *The Thomist* 44 (1980): a special issue of *Revue des sciences philosophiques et théologiques* 65 (1981), and M. Albert Hughes, *Albert the Great* (Oxford: Blackfriars, 1948) reprinted as a Supplement to *Spirituality Today* 39 (1987).

he was seen as an astonishing wonder of our age."[2] Centuries later, James Athanasius Weisheipl observed: "Not only was Albert the only man of the High Middle Ages to be called 'the Great,' but this title was used even before his death."[3]

A. Albert of Lauingen

Albert was born around 1200 in Lauingen near where the Danube has its source.[4] In 1223, he entered the Dominicans at the University of Padua. In his thirties he was the director of studies in several priories of friars in German lands. Around the age of forty he was sent to Paris to attain a doctorate. In 1245 he became the first Master of German origin at one of the European universities (in 1258 he signed a document of the university at Paris as *"frater Albertus Theutonicus* "[5]). In Paris where the texts of Aristotle and his Arab commentators were being studied enthusiastically, Albert became known for drawing students to their ideas. One of them was Thomas Aquinas. In 1248 Albert went to Cologne to start a school for the friars and others. With Thomas Aquinas as his assistant, Albert formed a house of studies for his Order. It was the first school of higher studies in Germany and the precursor of the Cologne University. Ludger Honnefelder has edited a volume of essays on the emergence of universities in Europe and the ole of Albert in their development.[6] Toward the end of 1249 Albert

---

[2] Cited in Joachim R. Söder, "Albert der Grosse – ein staunen-erregendes Wunder," *Albertus Magnus (1200-2000), Wort und Antwort* 41(2000): 145.

[3] Weisheipl, "Albertus Magnus,"Joseph Strayer, ed., *Dictionary of the Middle Ages* 1 (New York: Scribner, 1982) 129.

[4] Meinolf Lohrum, "Überlegungen zum Geburtsjahr Alberts des Grossen," W. Senner, ed., Omnia disce (Cologne: Wienand, 1996) 153-58; Adolf Layer and Max Springer, eds., *Albert von Lauingen. 700 Jahre + Albertus Magnus: Festschrift 1980* (Lauingen: Leo-Druck, 1980) holds essays on Albert's family and personality along with views on him by his contemporaries.

[5] H. Denifle, *Chartularium Universitatis Parisiensis* I (Paris: Delalain, 1889) 210.

[6] *Albertus Magnus und der Ursprung der Universitätsidee: die Begegnung der Wissenschaftskulturen im 13. Jahrhundert und die Entdeckung des Konzepts der Bildung durch Wissenschaft* (Berlin: Berlin University Press, 2011); Walther

began his enterprise of paraphrasing and commenting on Aristotle's works, "to make all the areas of philosophy intelligible to the Latins."[7] He was elected superior of the German province in 1254: its thirty-six priories reached from Strassburg on the Rhine to Rostock on the Baltic Sea. He subsequently attended general meetings of Dominicans in Milan, Paris, and Florence. In 1257 he resigned the provincialate and returned to Cologne to teach.

During those years he was sometimes engaged as a mediator – in Cologne and elsewhere -- in public disputes because not infrequently, bishop, mercantile class, and nobility found themselves at odds.[8] The particularly intense social and political conflict involving Albert in 1271 has been described in detail. His prominence in resolving disputes attracted the attention of Pope Alexander IV who appointed

---

Senner, " Albertus Magnus als Gründungsregens des Kölner Studium generale der Dominikaner," Jan Aertsen, ed., *Geistesleben im 13. Jahrhundert. Miscellanea mediaevalia* 27 (Berlin: De Gruyter, 2000) 129-169; Willehad Paul Eckert, "Albertus Magnus und das Studium generale der Dominikaner in Köln," *Geschichte in Köln. Studentische Zeitschrift am Historischen Seminar* 8 (1980): 16-45; H. C. Scheeben, "Albert der Große und Thomas von Aquin in Köln," *Divus Thomas* (Freiburg/Schweiz) 9 (1931): 28-34. The two Dominicans were present on August fifteenth at the solemn dedication of the corner stone of the new cathedral (Söder, "Albert der Grosse – ein staunenerregendes Wunder" 146).

[7] *Physica* Liber I, tractatus 1, capitulum 1 *Opera Omnia* IV, 1 (Münster: Aschendorff, 1987) 48-49.

[8] Hugo Stehkämper, "Albertus Magnus und die Kölner Sühne vom 17. April 1271," *Albertus Magnus (1200-1280), Wort und Antwort* 41 (2000): 170-73; see Manfred Groten, *Albertus Magnus und der Grosse Schied (Köln 1258) – Aristotelische Politik im Praxistest Lectio Albertina #12* (Münster: Aschendorff, 2011); J. A. Aertsen, ed., *Albert der Grosse in Köln* (Cologne: Presse- und Informationsstelle der Universität Köln, 1999); Meinolf Lohrum, *Albert der Grosse: Forscher-Lehrer-Anwalt des Friedens* (Mainz: Matthias-Grünewald, 1991); Manfred Groten, Albertus Magnus und der Grosse Schied (Köln 1258) – *Aristotelische Politik im Praxistest Lectio Albertina* #12 (Münster: Aschendorff, 2011).

him in 1260 bishop in Regensburg.[9] After he had reformed the clergy and reorganized the finances, in less than two years, he resigned that ministry and returned to teaching in Würzburg and Cologne where he died in 1280.

Yves Congar wrote eight years ago: "Albert believed in the mind. He perceived a profound harmony between the loftiness of divine life and the world of science and of finite human reasoning. This scholar, even as he argued for the autonomy of the sciences, had a special grasp of the reality of the unity of the universe. There exists one realm in which the facts of nature and the realities of grace are physically present."[10] Albert's research into the natural sciences[11] should not distract one from appreciating the theological project and goal of his thinking and of many of his writings. "Albert's plan can be grasped as a monumental synthesis considering all things in light of the varied revelation of God, a revelation appearing through Scripture and incarnation but also through creation."[12] Over the last fifteen years Henryk Anzulewicz has written articles on Albert to highlight the theological and unifying

[9] See Henryk Anzulewicz, "Albertus Magnus," Sebastian Cüppers, ed., *Kölner Theologen von Rupert von Deutz bis Wilhelm Nyssen* (Cologne: Marzellen, 2005) 30-68.

[10] Congar, "St. Albert the Great. The Power and the Anguish of the Intellectual Vocation," *Faith and Spiritual Life* (London: Darton, Longman & Todd, 1969) 65. This piece was originally written in 1931 to note the canonization of Albert: *Bulletin de St. Genevieve* (Novermber, 1931) 20-24.

[11] See Heinrich Balss, *Albertus Magnus als Zoologe* (Munich: Münchener Verlag, 1928); *Albertus Magnus als Biologe* (Stuttgart, Wissenschaftliche Verlagsgesellschaft, 1947). New studies on natural science and the Dominican include Michael Tkacz, "Albert the Great and the Revival of Aristotle's Zoological Research Program," *Vivarium* 45 (2007): 30-68 and "Albert the Great and the Aristotelian Reform of the Platonic Method of Division," *The Thomist* 73 (2009): 399-425; Henryk Anzulewicz, "Albertus Magnus und die Tiere," Sabine Obermaieer, ed., *Tiere und Fabelwesen im Mittelalter* (Berlin: De Gruyter, 2009) 29-54. Topics from the natural sciences include herbs and falcons, alchemy and human embryology.

[12] Söder, "Albert der Grosse – ein staunenerregendes Wunder" 164; see Georg Wieland, "Albert der Grosse. Der Entwurf einer eigenständigen Philosophie," *Philosophen des Mittelalters* (Darmstadt: Primus, 2000) 124-39.

themes of Albert's thought. He emphasizes the need to go beyond the past, limited view that Albert's originality lies in philosophy and science, and to see anew how theological principles and goals pervade his writings. Comprehending the thought-form of Albert the Great unfolds how his way of thinking treats the reality of being in a perspective both encompassing and unified. That perspective moves from its beginnings through a process of self-realization under the conditions of varied contingency to its ultimate goal, reflecting his underlying idea of life."[13] Human life, temporality, and all the causalities within creation contribute to this kind of structure, one seeking to explain the varied dimensions of life and time. Plato is present as well as Aristotle.[14] In Albert's writings "encompassing principles fashion a theological structure" as "a unified and complete system offering a total explanation of all the reality of being."[15] Breadth marks Albert's thought in various ways. "Perhaps the medieval conception of a universal complex of various sciences, a university, existing in a unity inclusive of all, found its broadest expression in the structure of the teaching of that universal teacher."[16]

---

[13] Anzulewicz, "Die Denkstruktur des Albertus Magnus. Ihre Dekodierung und ihre Relevanz für die Begrifflichkeit und Terminologie," J. Hamesse and C. Steel, eds., L'élaboration du vocabulaire philosophique au Moyen Âge (Turnhout: Brepols, 2000) 369-96; "Die Rekonstruktion der Denkstruktur des Albertus Magnus. Skizze und Thesen eines Forschungsprojektes," Theologie und Glaube 90 (2000): 606-11; "Zwischen Faszination und Ablehnung: Theologie und Philosophie im 13 Jh. in ihrem Verhältnis zueinander," M. Olszewski, ed., What is "Theology" in the Middle Ages? Religious Cultures of Europe (11th – 15th Centuries) as Reflected in Their Self-Understanding (Münster: Aschendorff, 2007) 129-165.

[14] Anzulewicz, "Die platonische Tradition bei Albertus Magnus. Eine Hinführung," S. Gersh and M. J. F. M. Hoenen, eds., The Platonic Tradition in the Middle Ages. A Doxographic Approach (Berlin: De Gruyter, 2002) 207-227.

[15] Anzulewicz, "Albertus Magnus – Der Denker des Ganzen," Wort und Antwort 41 (2000): 154.

[16] Söder, "Albert der Grosse – ein staunenerregendes Wunder" 146.

B. Albert's Writings

Mention should be made first of editions of Albert's works. A collection of Albert's writings was edited and published in thirty-eight volumes by Auguste Borgnet in the nineteenth century.[17] That Latin text was based somewhat on an earlier edition in twenty-one volumes by Pierre Jammy, *B. Alberti Magnis, Ratisb. Ep., O.P., Opera*.[18] The Albertus-Magnus-Institut, founded in 1931 by the Archdiocese of Cologne with its present location in Bonn, has been editing for some years a critical text of Albert's writings: Alberti Magni, *Opera Omnia* (Editio Coloniensis). For that series twenty-eight volumes out of a planned forty-one are listed as having already appeared, while six are in proximate preparation. The institute's website describes its library, lectures, publications, and projects.[19]

C. Four Recent Publications

Four publications have stimulated this survey: Irven M. Resnick & Kenneth F. Kitchell, Jr., *Albert the Great: A Selectively Annotated Bibliography (1900 - 2000)*;[20] Walter Senner, ed., *Albertus Magnus. Zu Gedenken nach 800 Jahre: Neue Zugänge, Aspekte und Perspektiven*;[21] from the Albertus-Magnus-Institut in Bonn there are two series --

---

[17] (Paris: Vivès, 1890-1897). Bruno Tremblay (Department of Philosophy, St. Jerome's University, Waterloo, Ontario, Canada) has placed on line the entire Borgnet Edition; see the website,"Alberti Magni e-corpus."

[18] (Lyons: Prost, 1651).

[19] See Ludger Honnefelder, Mechthild Dreyer, *Albertus Magnus und die Editio Coloniensis*, Lectio Albertina #1 (Münster: Aschendorff, 1999) and Bernd Göring, "Zur Überlieferung der Werke Alberts des Grossen – von der Handschrift bis zur modernen Überlieferung," *Wort und Antwort* 41 (2000): 186-89. One finds electronic resources under "Albert the Great – Links" or "Albertus-Magnus-Institut Bonn" and lited in Irven M. Resnick & Kenneth F. Kitchell, Jr., "Introduction," *Albert the Great: A Selectively Annotated Bibliography (1900 - 2000)* (Tempe: Arizona Center for Medieval and Renaissance Studies, 2004) xi.

[20] (Tempe: Arizona Center for Medieval and Renaissance Studies, 2004).

[21] (Akademie: Berlin, 2001).

Lectio Albertina[22] and *Subsidia Albertina;* finally there is a special issue of *Wort und Antwort.*[23]

Albert the Great: A Selectively Annotated Bibliography (1900 – 2000) by Resnick and Kitchell is a volume of over four hundred pages. The editors point out that bibliographical resources on Albert are few and often inaccessible in North America. This bibliography includes 2576 entries, and there is an index of names and subjects occupying thirty pages. "The print version of this bibliography should appeal to scholars who enjoy the leisure necessary to examine carefully the extensive literature on Albert."[24] Books and articles are gathered into nineteen sections, ranging from "Albert's Life and Works" and "Iconography and Albert in Art" to "Theology – General" and "Albertism." Some individual articles and books are summarized.

In terms of bibliographies from the past there have been partial bibliographies like the one assembled in 1931 by Yves Congar for the issue of the *Revue Thomiste* celebrating the canonization of Albert[25] or those in volumes celebrating in 1980 the seven hundredth anniversary of his death. Those bibliographies were followed by G. Krieger's survey of literature from 1973 to 1988.[26] There is also an on-going electronic bibliography: Jörgen Vijgen, "Albertus Magnus – A Selective Bibliography," Nederlands Thomas Genootschap (www. thomisme.org). The Albertus-Magnus-Institute in Bonn now offers an "Online Edition of the Works of Saint Albert the Great" to private individuals and to institutions.[27]

---

[22] (Münster: Aschendorff, 1999 - 2006).

[23] *Albertus Magnus (1200-2000), Wort und Antwort* 41: 4 (Oktober/ Dezember, 2000).

[24] Resnick, Kitchell, "Introduction," xii.

[25] Congar, "Essai de Bibliographie Albertinienne," *Revue Thomiste* 31 (1931): 422-68.

[26] Krieger, "Albertus Magnus. Veröffentlichungen in den Jahren 1973-1988," G. Fløistad, ed., *Philosophy and Science in the Middle Ages* (Boston: Kluwer, 1990) 241-59.

[27] *Alberti Magni Opera Omnia.* Editio Digitalis (Münster: Aschendorff, 2011).

Walter Senner's volume holds seven hundred pages of essays. Philosophical studies treat old and new topics like the world of nature or the relationship of Albert to Arab philosophy, while in the last two sections there are essays on the Trinity, biblical hermeneutics, papal primacy, predestination, prayer and mysticism, and women's religious movements. This volume is a contemporary witness to Albert's breadth of interests and to the breadth of contemporary research.[28] Irven M. Resnick has expanded his research further through the volume of essays: *A Companion to Albert the Great* (Leiden: Brill, 2013).

The series *Lectio Albertina* from the Albertus-Magnus-Institut in Bonn is a series of scholarly monographs, now numbering twelve. One of them by Rudolf Schieffer on "Mendicancy and Theology in Conflict with Episcopacy" explores the papal appointment of Albert to the bishopric of Regensburg, his activities there, and his decision to resign after less than two years.[29] The choice by the pope of Albert as bishop was caused by financial and ecclesiastical problems in the diocese of Regensburg (his appointment is an early example of papal appointment of bishops in Germany). In less than two years Albert saw that the diocese would be capable of selecting a moral and competent successor, and he returned to his work as teacher and writer, remaining, of course, a bishop. Schieffer's documentary study of Albert's time as bishop critiques legends about Albert written down after the end of the fourteenth century. The Bonn Institut has begun a second series: *Subsidia Albertina,* where there has appeared a volume

---

[28] Senner's writings on Albert (for instance, "Zur Definition der Wahrheit bei Albertus Magnus," Thomas Eggensberg, ed., *Wahrheit: Recherchen zwischen Hochscholastik und Postmoderne* [Mainz: Matthias-Grünewald, 1995] 11-48) are numerous. Related to the Senner volume is Ludger Honnefelder et al., *Albertus Magnus und die Anfänge der Aristoteles-Rezeption im lateinischen Mittelalter* (Münster: Aschendorff, 2005) where studies on Aristotle's philosophy and its entrance into the West in the twelfth and thirteenth centuries lead to essays on Albert himself. Ingrid Craemer-Ruegenberg's *Albertus Magnus* has been issued in a revised edition by Henryk Anzulewicz (Leipzig: St. Benno, 2005); it has sections on Albert's influence and bibliographies.

[29] *Albertus Magnus. Mendikantentum und Theologie im Widerstreit mit dem Bischofsamt. Lectio Albertina* #3 (Münster: Aschendorff, 1999).

of essays presenting the progress in research on Albert in the past two decades, *Via Alberti. Texte-Quellen-Interpretationen.*[30]

A fourth resource is the special issue of *Wort und Antwort* with essays on Albert ranging from eschatology to art. Related to this is an issue of *Listening* on *St. Albert the Great and Dominican Teaching.* There are essays by M. Mulchahey on the Studium at Cologne and early Dominican education, W. Senner on Albert and Meister Eckhart, and by T. J. White on Albert and modern views of Wisdom.[31]

D. Earlier Writings on Albert

For the English-speaking world an early source from the 1930s was Hieronymous Wilms, *Albert the Great. Saint and Doctor of the Church,*[32] and around the same time the journal *Blackfriars* published M.-D. Chenu, "The Revolutionary Intellectualism of St. Albert the Great."[33] Volumes celebrated the canonization of Albert in 1931 (he had been beatified in 1622). For that event the *Revue Thomiste* issued a special number with historical essays by Angelus Walz and Pierre Mandonnet and theological essays like those on the gifts of the Holy Spirit by Benoit Lavaud and on predestination by Réginald Garrigou-Lagrange.[34] *Divus Thomas* published a "St. Albertus-Magnus-

---

[30] Ludger Honnefelder, Hannes Möhle, Susana Bullido del Barrio, eds., *Via Alberti. Texte-Quellen-Interpretationen* (Münster: Aschendorff, 2009). An Australian journal has published three essays on Albert and education: Gabrielle Kelly, Kevin Saunders, eds., *Dominican Approaches in Education: Towards the Intelligent Use of Liberty* (Adelaide: Australian Theological Forum, 2007).

[31] *Listening* 43: 3 (2008).

[32] (London: Burns, Oates & Washbourne, 1933).

[33] *Blackfriars* 19 (1938): 5-15.

[34] *Revue Thomiste* 36 (1931); see Mandonnet, "Albert le Grand et Thomas d'Aquin," "Frères Prêcheurs (La théologie dans l'Ordre des)," *Dictionnaire de théologie catholique* 6 (Paris: Letouzey et Ané, 1924) 872-74. On the gifts of the Holy Spirit in Albert's theology see Bavo M. van Hulse, "De leer over de gaven van de H. Geest bij den h. Albertus den Groote," *Bijdragen* 5 (1942): 1-78.

Festschrift" opening with a letter by Pius XI and a forward by Andreas Cardinal Frühwirth, O.P. That volume held studies on Albert and modern philosophy, political science, geology, the procession of the Holy Spirit, and the eucharist.[35] Earlier in 1928 Martin Grabmann had published a lengthy article of a hundred pages on Albert and his age.[36]

E. Albert and Some Theological Topics.

The volumes by Senner and by Manfred Entrich[37] hold studies on the theological and exegetical methods of Albert: Karl Cardinal Lehmann's essay treats the synthesis of faith and knowing in Albert, and Mikolaj Olszewski's looks at his theory of biblical interpretation."[38] Lehmann also published in the *Lectio Albertina* a monograph treating Albert's idea of theology, and Walter Senner offers there a lengthy survey of Albert's major works in terms of the relationship of theology and philosophy and in terms of the affective and speculative directions in theology.[39] Albert distinguished science

---

[35] *Divus Thomas* 9 (1931); 10 (1932).

[36] "Der Einfluss Alberts des Grossen auf das mittelalterliche Geistesleben," *Zeitschrift für katholische Theologie* 52 (1928): 156-256; see Grabmann, *Der hl. Albert der Grosse. Ein wissenschaftliches Charakterbild mit Bild* (Munich: Max Hueber, 1932).

[37] Manfred Entrich, ed., *Albertus Magnus. Sein Leben und seine Bedeutung* (Graz: Styria, 1982); the volume holds essays by Karl Meyer, Isnard Frank, and others.

[38] In Senner, *Albertus Magnus*; see too Giuseppe Ferraro, "L'esegesi dei testi pneumatologici nelle 'Enarrationes in Joannem' di Sant' Alberto Magno," *Angelicum* 60 (1983): 40-79; Andrew Hofer, "He taught us how to fly: Albert the Great on John the Evangelist," *Angelicum* 87 (2010): 569-89.

[39] Lehmann, *Zum Begriff der Theologie bei Albertus Magnus. Lectio Albertina* #8 (Münster: Aschendorff, 2006); Senner, *Alberts des Grossen Verständnis von Theologie und Philosophie, Lectio Albertina* #9 (Münster: Aschendorff, 2009). See too Hannes Möhle, "Zum Verhältnis von Theologie und Philosophie bei Albert dem Grossen: Wissenschaftstheoretische Reflexionen während der Gründung des Studium generale in Köln," Siegfried Schmidt, ed., *Rhenisch-Kölnisch-Katholisch: Beiträge zur Kirchen- und Landesgeschichte sowie zur Geschichte des Buch- und Bibliothekswesens der Rhinelande* (Cologne: Libelli Rhenani, 2008) 146-162.

clearly from religion and sought a variety of methodologies for the sciences. Joachim Söder, Anzulewicz, and others have described with a new depth Albert's anthropology.[40] Ruth Meyer inquired into Albert's contribution to a post-modern age, for he spoke of sciences that would be discovered in the future and noted how questions on the boundaries of diverse disciplines were difficult.[41]

To peruse the bibliography of writings on Albert by Resnick and Kitchell is to notice that philosophical themes have been studied more frequently than religious ones. Nonetheless, recent years witness a marked increase in theological essays. Gilles Emery has written on Albert's theology of the Trinity, while there is no lack of studies for a philosophy of God.[42] In the area of Christology there were studies from the 1930s on the hypostatic union by Vincent-Marie Pollet and Ferdinand Haberl, while later decades saw essays on Christology by Stephen Hipp, Donald Goergen, and others.[43] Aspects of the theology of

---

[40] See Anzulewicz, "Anthropology: The Concept of Man in Albert the Great," in I. M. Resnick, ed., *A Companion to Albert the Great* (Leiden: Brill, 2013) 325-346; "Der anthropologieentwurf des Albertus Magnus und die Frage nach dem Begriff und wissenschafts-systematischen Ort einer mittelalterlichen Anthropologie," Jan A. Aertsen, Andreas Speer, eds., *Was ist Philosophie im Mittelalter?* (New York: De Gruyter: 1998) 765-68; "Zur Theorie des menschlichen Lebens nach Albertus Magnus. Theologische Grundlegungen und ihre bioethischen Implikationen," *Studia Mediewistyczne* 33 (1998): 35-49; "Die Anthropologie des Albertus Magnus als Ort des Dialogs zwischen den Sancti und philosophi," Frano Prcela, ed., Dialog. *Auf dem Weg zur Wahrheit und zum Glauben* (Zagreb: Globus, 1996) 47-52

[41] Söder, "Der Mensch als Ganzheit. Alberts anthropologischer Entwurf," *Wort und Antwort* 41 (2000): 159-64; Meyer, "Versöhnte Verschiedenheit. Zur Wissenschaftskonzeption bei Albertus Magnus," *Wort und Antwort* 41 (2000): 165-169. see Georg Wieland, *Zwischen Natur und Vernunft. Alberts des Grossen Begriff vom Menschen* (Münster: Aschendorff, 1999).

[42] Emery, *La Trinité Créatrice. Trinité et la création dans les commentaires aux Sentences de Thomas d'Aquin et de ses précurseurs Albert le Grand et Bonaventure* (Paris: Vrin, 1995); Alain de Libera, "Toute-puissance et théodicée. Albert le Grand," O. Boulnois, ed., *La Puissance et son Ombre: de Pierre Lombard à Luther* (Paris: Aubier, 1994) 141-68.

[43] Pollet, "L'union hypostatique d'après saint Albert le Grand," *Revue Thomiste* 38 (1933): 505-32, 689-724; Haberl, *Die Inkarnationslehre des heiligen*

grace have attracted some writers: Réginald Garrigou-Lagrange and
Klaus Obenauer on predestination, Yves Congar on sanctifying grace,
Thomas O'Meara on justification, and Patrizia Conforti on the grace of
union.[44] Two early works on grace are Herbert Doms, *Die Gnadenlehre
des seligen Alberti Magni* and Josef Goergen, *Des hl. Albertus Magnus
Lehre von der göttlichen Vorsehung und dem Fatum.*[45]

To continue surveying theological areas, sacrament is also a theme
for studies on Albert. A monograph from the Bonn series treats
transubstantiation in the eucharist in light of Albert's views, focusing
on an arrival of Aristotelian conceptuality and with metaphysical
problems posed by the perdurance of the appearances in the
sacrament.[46] Thomas McGonigle wrote on the medieval context of

---

Albertus Magnus (Freiburg: Herder, 1939); Goergen, "Albert the Great and
Thomas Aquinas on the Motive of the Incarnation," *The Thomist* 44 (1980):
523-538; Hipp, *"Person" in Christian Tradition and in the Conception of Saint
Albert the Great: A Systematic Study of its Concept as Illuminated by the
Mysteries of the Trinity and the Incarnation* (Münster: Aschendorff, 2001); see
Corey Barnes, "Albert the Great and Thomas Aquinas on Person, Hypostasis,
and Hypostatic Union," *Thomist* 72 (2008): 107-46.

[44] Garrigou-Lagrange, "La volonté salvifique et la prédestination chez le
Bienheureux Albert le Grand," *Revue Thomiste* 36 (1931): 371-85; Obenauer,
"Zur Prädestinationslehre des hl. Albertus Magnus," Senner, *Albertus Magnus*;
Congar, "Albert le Grand théologien de la grâce sanctifiante," *Vie Spirituelle* 34
(1933): 109-40; Hugo Amico, *On the Justification of the Sinner according to St.
Albert the Great and a Comparison with the Doctrine of St. Thomas and the
Tridentine Council* (Rome: The Angelicum, 1954); O'Meara, "Albert the Great
and Martin Luther on Justification," *The Thomist* 44 (1980): 539-59; Conforti,
"La doctrine de la grace d'union et son evolution chez Albert le Grand et ses
contemporains," Senner, *Albertus Magnus*. On sin see Albert Stohr, "Zur
Erbsündenlehre Alberts des Grossen," Albert Lang et al., eds., *Aus der
Geisteswelt des Mittelalters* (Münster: Aschendorff, 1935) 627-50.

[45] (Breslau: Müller und Seiffert, 1929); (Vechta: Albertus-Magnus-Verlag,
1932).

[46] Hans Jorissen, *Der Beitrag Alberts des Grossen zur theologischen Rezeption
des Aristoteles am Beispiel der Transsubstantionslehre, Lectio Albertina* #5
(Münster: Aschendorff, 2002); Jorissen, "Materie und Form der Sakramente
im Verständnis Alberts des Grossen," *Zeitschrift für katholische Theologie* 80
(1958): 267-315.

Albert's sacramental theology where the Dominican seeks to reconcile theologies of the sacraments from Augustine, Peter Lombard, and Hugh of St. Victor, while David Wright presented Albert's interpretation of the rites of the Mass according to historical, moral, and mystical meanings of the words and actions in contrast to allegorical interpretations like that of Lothar of Segni.[47] Franz-Josef Nocke's book, after treating the idea of sacrament in general, turns to the two sacraments of penance and marriage. They are of particular interest because in the view of some medieval writers laypersons can administer them, a position that interests Albert.[48] At the beginning of the twentieth century Georg Gromer composed a survey of medieval theologies on laypersons hearing a sacramental confession, and he placed the thinking of Albert as climactic among those affirming this activity, for he sketched a number of ways in which sins can be absolved among the baptized through faith and love and concluded that laypeople hearing confessions is a true sacrament. "With Albert the theory of lay confession stands at its highest level of expression. Essentially the effect is the same as confession to a priest."[49]

For Albert's ecclesiology one can find an orientation in Yves Congar, *L'Église de Saint Augustin à l'époque moderne*.[50] Aspiring to unite Plato and Aristotle, hierarchy and people, Albert wrote of the Body of Christ as both church and eucharist. Each Christian is personally joined to Christ through the Body of the church. The Holy Spirit is the ultimate

---

[47] The articles by McGonigle and Wright are found in *The Thomist* 44 (1980): 560-83 and 584-96; see Ludwig Hödl, "Der dogmatische Begriff der sakramentalen Konzelebration in der scholastischen Theologie des 13. und 14. Jahrhunderts," *Zeitschrift für katholische Theologie* 127 (2005): 361-90.

[48] Franz-Josef Nocke, *Sakrament und personaler Vollzug bei Albertus Magnus* (Münster: Aschendorff, 1967); on baptism there is Alfons Müller, *Die Lehre von der Taufe bei Albert dem Grossen* (Munich: Schöningh, 1967).

[49] Georg Gromer, *Die Laienbeicht im Mittelalter. Ein Beitrag zu ihrer Geschichte* (Munich: Lentner, 1909) 43; see Franz Gillmann, "Zur Frage der Laienbeicht," *Der Katholik* 1 (1909): 435-51.

[50] (Paris: Cerf, 1970) 230-32; see *Congar, A History of Theology* (New York: Doubleday, 1968) 104-14. Treating Albert's ecclesiology is Wilhelm Scherer, *Des seligen Albertus Magnus Lehre von der Kirche* (Freiburg: Herder, 1928).

principle of church unity as well as of activity and office. There is a distinction between the members of the church and the members of the Body of Christ which is a congregation of love.

Albert gave papal office and authority sparse consideration. Already in 1872 Franz Xaver Leitner had touched on Albert's views of the papacy in a study on Aquinas and infallibility.[51] Ulrich Horst's analysis of papal office stresses that Albert understood the office of the bishop of Rome mainly in terms of administration and jurisdiction; the pope held in a limited way aspects of universal jurisdiction and leadership but enjoyed only to a modest extent the role of teacher.[52] Anzulewicz has written on the role of the fathers of the church in Albert's ecclesiology and on his understanding of the church as a society. "From its origins and through its salvific work in unity with Christ the head of the 'corpus mysticum,' the church transcends the limitations of time, space, and matter. Within the conditions of being a *viator* and living through faith (and not through immediate vision) the church participates in the glory of God. It is the house of God and of the Spirit; it is a created work like the human being. Consequently it has a double reality with transcendent and contingent dimensions: on the one hand, the mystical Body vitalized by the Holy Spirit...and on the other hand, a unified community of faith with a leader who is the successor of Peter and who leads all the members."[53]

---

[51] *Der hl. Thomas von Aquin über das unfehlbare Lehramt des Papstes* (Freiburg: Herder, 1872) 177-81.

[52] Ulrich Horst, "Albertus Magnus und Thomas von Aquin zu Matthäus 16:18f. Ein Beitrag zur Lehre vom päpstlichen Primat," Senner, *Albertus Magnus* 553-71; see Edward P. Mahoney, "Albert the Great on Christ and Hierarchy," Kent Emery and Joseph Wawrykow, eds., *Christ among the Medieval Dominicans* (Notre Dame: University of Notre Dame Press, 1998) 364-92. Anzulewicz describes Albert's theology of minor orders, major orders including priesthood, and religious life in "Priestertum und Ordensstand nach Albertus Magnus," Thomas Prügl and Marianne Schlosser, eds., *Kirchenbild und Spiritualität* (Paderborn: Schöningh, 2007) 63-86.

[53] Anzulewicz, "Zum Kirchenverständnis des Albertus Magnus," in R. M. W. Stammberger et al, eds., *"Das Haus Gottes, das seid ihr selbst." Mittelalterliches und barockes Kirchenverständnis im Spiegel der Kirchweihe* (Berlin: Akademie, 2006) 356; see "Die Kirche als Mystischer Leib Christi. Zur Bedeutung der

To turn to the realm of pastoral activity, essays on Albert as a bishop and mediator show him to be a person of both administrative and pastoral gifts. Congar studied the efforts of the Dominican community as a "team" where the Friars Preachers' intellectual apostolate was realized by men with varied expertise and ministries.[54] Manfred Entrich has written on Albert's medieval pastoral plan for religious education.[55] There are essays on prayer and movements of religious women in Albert's view as well as on forms of popular devotion to Albert.[56] Simon Tugwell has published an analysis of Albert's spirituality along with texts illustrating it.[57]

Albert's eschatology has attracted attention: resurrection, the death of Jesus, purgative fire, and German piety in the face of death. Anzulewicz offers an essay on the finitude of creation, the omnipresence of time, and the role of fire in destruction and transformation. "In his philosophical writings Albert does not discuss the

---

Rezeption der Kirchenväter für die Entwicklung des Kirchenverständnisses im Frühwerk des Albertus Magnus," J. Arnold et al., eds., *Väter der Kirche. Ekklesiales Denken von den Anfängen bis in die Neuzeit* (Paderborn:Schöningh, 2003) 687-715.

[54] *"'In Dulcedine societatis quaerere veritatem.'* Notes sur le travail en équipe chez S. Albert et chez les Prêcheurs au XIIIe siècle," Gerbert Meyer and Albert Zimmermann, eds., *Albertus Magnus. Doctor Universalis*, 1280/1980, 47-57.

[55] *Die Bergpredigt als Ausbildungsordnung: der katechetische Entwurf einer 'ratio formationis' bei Albert dem Grossen* (Würzburg: Echter, 1992); see Stanley B. Cunningham, *Reclaiming Moral Agency. The Moral Philosophy of Albert the Great* (Washington, D.C.: The Catholic University of America Press, 2008); Jörn Müller, *Natürliche Moral und philosophische Ethik bei Albertus Magnus* (Münster: Aschendorff, 2001); Anzulewicz, "Zur Theorie des menschlichen Lebens nach Albertus Magnus. Theologische Grundlegungen und ihre bioethischen Implikationen," *Studia Mediewistyczne* 33 (1998): 35-49.

[56] Entrich, *Albertus Magnus. Gebete zu ihm, Gebete von ihm* (Cologne: St. Andreas, 1979); see the essays listed under "Mysticism" in Resnick, Kitchell, 317-19.

[57] Simon Tugwell, *Albert and Thomas. Selected Writings* (New York: Paulist Press, 1988).

end of the world because he cannot assume with purely rational principles that this world has an end. Biblical revelation tells him that the world had a beginning (this is at the same time the beginning of time) and that it will have an end....This world must have an end and must experience a renewal because in its origins it was more perfect and because it strives towards renewal."[58] The universe's term is not a consequence of the process of nature but results from the external and unique cause of the total reality of the universe. The process of renewal begins with periods of destruction by fire at lower levels and moves to higher levels where fire becomes illumination, holiness, and vision.[59]

F. Representations of Albert in Art

Erhard Schlieter offers a survey of how Albert is presented in art over the centuries.[60] In 1980 an exhibition on Albert in art was assembled in Cologne for which Hugo Stehkämper wrote an introduction.[61] *Albertus Magnus, der grosse Neugierige* is an illustrated guide to an exhibit held in Regensburg in 2002, a colorful, brief

---

[58] Anzulewicz, "Ende und Erneuerung der Welt," *Wort und Antwort* 41 (2000): 183; see Albert, *De Homine* (Hamburg: Felix Meiner, 2004); Albert, *Liber de natura et origine animae* (Freiburg: Herder, 2006).

[59] See Jeffrey P. Hergan, *St. Albert the Great's Theory of the Beatific Vision* (New York: Lang, 2002). Caroline Walker Bynum treats Albert in *The Resurrection of the Body in Western Christianity* (New York: Columbia University Press, 1995) 255-71.

[60] "Albertus Magnus in der Kunst," *Wort und Antwort* 41 (2000): 174-79; see essays in Adolf Layer and Max Springer, eds., *Albert von Lauingen. Siebenhundert Jahre Albertus Magnus* (Lauingen: Hist. Ver. Dillingen a. d. Donau, 1980) and Genoveva Nitz, *Albertus Magnus in der Volkskunst. Die Alberti-Tafeln* (Munich: Schnell & Steiner, 1980).

[61] Hugo Stehkämper and Matthias Zender, *Albertus Magnus. Auststellung zum 700 Todestag* (Cologne: Historisches Archiv der Stadt Köln, 1980); W. Senner, *Blühende Gelehrsamkeit. Eine Ausstellung zur Gründung des Studium Generale der Dominikaner in Köln vor 750 Jahren* (Cologne: Kölner Stadtmuseum, 1998); see Anzulewicz, "Albertus Magnus und die moderne Kunst," *Archiv für mittelalterliche Philosophie und Kultur* 14 (2008): 28-45.

presentation of the many sides of Albert.[62] Further studies on this topic are listed in the section on "Iconography and Albert in Art" in Resnick and Kitchell.

G. The Influence of Albert

Scholars speak of "Albertism," the influence of Albert in subsequent decades and centuries. Does this imply a school at Cologne or a movement beginning there? Resnick and Kitchell arrange articles around three special figures who may have been influenced by Albert in some way: Dante, Meister Eckhart,[63] and Galileo. Then their bibliography offers ten pages listing articles on wider movements and important disciples. Alain de Libera has published a number of studies on Albert and his disciples. *Albert le Grand et la philosophie* surveys current research before turning to Albert's treatment of philosophy, God and being, a dynamic metaphysics, and a theological psychology of mind.[64] This book presents the influence of Albert on major thinkers of the following generation like Ulrich of Strassburg and Dietrich of Freiburg. "Even as bishop of Regensburg and as professor at the University of Paris, Albert the Great was not the only mentor of his German confreres in philosophy, science, and theology. He did, however, exercise a marked influence on the theology and spirituality

---

[62] *Albertus Magnus, Begegnungen in Regensburg* (Regensburg: Stadt-Regensburg, 2002).

[63] Ideas on Albert and Eckhart are presented by Kurt Flasch, *Meister Eckhart. Die Geburt der "Deutschen Mystik" aus dem Geist der arabischen Philosophie* (Munich: Beck, 2006).

[64] (Paris: Vrin, 1990); see also *Métaphysique et noétique: Albert le Grand* (Paris: Vrin, 2005); "Albert le Grand, 1200 – 1280," Claude Gauvard et al, eds., *Dictionnaire du Moyen Âge* (Paris: Presses universitaires de France, 2002) 26-29. There is a collection of essays on this area by Maarten Hoenen and Alain de Libera, *Albertus Magnus und der Albertismus. Deutsche philosophische Kultur des Mittelalters* (Leiden: Brill, 1995); see Ruedi Imbach and Christoph Flüeler, *Albert der Grosse und die deutsche Dominikanerschule* (Fribourg: Universitätsverlag, 1985); Hans Gerhard Senger, "Der Kölner Albertismus," *Albertus Magnus in Köln* (Köln: Universitätsverlag, 1999) 43-55. Anzulewicz has assembled a bibliography of writings on Albert's influence in the fifteenth century, *Albertus Magnus* 211-12.

of his Dominican province to which he gave impressive Neo-Platonic, Dionysian,[65] and Avicennan forms (more and more articles are devoted to Albert's relationships to Arabic commentators on Aristotle[66]). Aertsen writes of a dynamic conjunction of Arab thought, Dionysian theology, and Albert's own perspectives resulting in a transcendental science.[67]

The expression 'a Dominican school of Cologne' stands for a number of influences and a number of persons active in writing and teaching. There was a mutual interaction in terms of books and people that formed a network or terrain for Rhenish mysticism.[68] Experts describe

---

[65] See Thierry-Dominique Humbrecht, "Albert le Grand, Commentateur de la *Théologie Mystique* de Denys," *Revue des sciences philosophiques et théologiques* 90 (2006): 225-71. Édouard-Henri Wéber has edited Albert's commentary on the *Mystical Theology* of Dionysius: *Saint Albert le Grand, Commentaire de la 'Théologie Mystique' de Denys le Pseudo-Aréopagite* (Paris: Cerf, 1993); Maria Burger, "Das Verhältnis von Philosophie und Theologie in den Dionysius-Kommentaren Alberts des Grossen," Jan A. Aertsen, Andreas Speer, eds., *Was ist Philosophie im Mittelalter?* 579-586; Anzulewicz, "Pseudo-Dionysius Areopagita und das Strukturprinzip des Denkens von Albert dem Grossen," A. Speer et al, eds., *Die Dionysius-Rezeption im Mittelalter* (Turnhout: Brepols, 2000) 251-95; "Rezeption und Reinterpretation: Pseudo-Dionysius Areopagita, die Peripatetiker und die Umdeutung der augustinishcen Illuminationslehre bei Albertus Magnus," Ulrich Köpf and Dieter Bauer, eds., *Kulturkontakte und Rezeptionsvorgänge in der Theologie des 12.und 13. Jahrhunderts* (Münster, Aschendorff, 2011) 103-126; Walter Senner, *Alberts des Grossen Verständnis von Theologie und Philosophie,* 13-26.

[66] Kurt Flasch, "Albert der Grosse, Öffnung zur arabischen Welt," *Meister Eckhart. Die Geburt der "Deutschen Mystik" aus dem Geist der arabischen Philosophie* (Munich: Beck, 2006) 67-85.

[67] Aertsen, "Albertus Magnus und die mittelalterliche Philosophie" 111-28.

[68] Alain de Libera, *L'Introduction à la mystique Rhénane d'Albert le Grand à Maître Eckhart* (Paris: O.E.I.L., 1984) 10; see Loris Sturlese, *Die deutsche Philosophie im Mittelalter. Von Bonifatius bis zu Albert dem Grossen 748-1280* (Munich: Beck, 1993) and *Vernunft und Glück: Die Lehre vom 'intellectus adeptus' und die mentale Glückseligkeit bei Albert dem Grossen* (Münster: Aschendorff, 2005); Craemer-Ruegenberg and Anzulewicz, "Zur Wirkungsgeschichte der Philosophie Alberts des Grossen," *Albertus Magnus* 166-78.

this intellectual milieu as a speculative mysticism, a metaphysical mysticism, or a mysticism of essence of which all are a metaphysics of the Word. De Libera has focused on the mystical dimension in the thought of the Cologne school. "Rhenish theology is the theology of Rhenish mysticism: there is its place of discussion, its school of discussion, and its product. This is the theology that comes from Albert, and it is not totally a German theology."[69]

* * *

A comment from Alain de Libera on Albert's influence in theology and mysticism offers a conclusion for this survey. Albert is not simply a stage prior to Thomas Aquinas or a version of Avicenna. Albert has his own originality, and his works are not paraphrases or syntheses of the texts of others. "The 'paradigm of Albert' has its coherence, its proper horizon, its particular objects...Albert's theology is not an alternative to Thomism. We need to forget Thomas and face directly -- without intermediaries or codes habitually used to describe Albert -- the real philosophical project of Albert. This project, born at Paris and reaching maturity at Cologne, had an epochal importance."[70]

Today books and articles are researching and thereby spotlighting the theology of Albert of Lauingen. There is much to discover in his thought and not a little to be learned from it. He was an independent scholar and believer — independent in the birth of a new age, independent in science and in faith, independent in political turmoil and in church life.

---

[69] Alain de Libera, *L'Introduction à la mystique Rhénane* 11.

[70] Alain de Libera, Raison et Foi. *Archéologie d'une crise d'Albert le Grand à Jean-Paul II* (Paris; Seuil, 2003) 82.

Alain de Libera

Albert the Great, 1200 – 1280

Born toward 1200 and entering the Friars Preachers in 1223 or 1229 after studies in Padua and Cologne, Albert the Great (Albertus Magnus, Albert von Lauingen) is the first German to have obtained the degree of master in theology from the University of Paris after his study there from 1245 to 1248). His long career included the varied activities of a Dominican intellectual during the "scholastic age." He taught in the Dominican studium of Cologne where he had as students Thomas Aquinas (until 1252) and Ulrich of Strasbourg. He was provincial of the Dominican Province of Teutonia from 1254 to 1257 and bishop of Regensburg in 1260. He preached the crusade "in Germany, Bohemia, and other countries where the language was German" at the express wish of Pope Urban IV. He completed his life in Cologne in 1280 after some further periods of teaching in Würzburg (1264) and Strasbourg (1267). Canonized by Pius XI in 1931 he was named patron of the natural sciences by Pius XII in 1941.

Albert the Great has been viewed at times as a philosopher influencing theology negatively. This reproach is found in the *Tricelogium astrologiae theologizatae* of Gerson and later in the eighteenth century in the *Historia critica philosophiae* of Johann Jakob Brucker and then with Diderot who wrote: "No one understood better the Aristotelian dialectic and metaphysics. But he drew into theology subtleties which furthered its corruption." A number of "biographies" from the late Middle Ages treated him. Written about 1300 the *Legenda I* (today lost) was used by Henry of Herford around 1355; there is from 1414 a *Vita domini et magistri Alberti Magni* by Louis of Valladolid. Around 1421 (or 1483-87) the *Legenda Coloniensis* was written, and a little later Peter of Prussia composed his *Vita b. Alberti Magni,* while in 1488 or 1490 Rudolf of Nijmegen issued his *Legenda litteralis Alberti Magni.* It is only in 1880 after the work of Georg Freiherr von Hertling that the scientific study of the life and works of the teacher of Thomas Aquinas was pursued: for instance, by Paul von Loë (1901-02) and Heribert Christian Scheeben (1931). The publications of Bruno Nardi firmly placed him in the spotlight.

The first scholastic to interpret the totality of the writings of Aristotle then accessible, Albert left a monumental corpus: it covers on an encyclopedic scale all the areas of knowledge in philosophy and theology. In terms of philosophy, the teacher of Cologne treats logic, physics and cosmology, meteorology and mineralogy, psychology and noetics, natural sciences and zoology, and in terms of philosophy there are works on politics, ethics, and metaphysics. In theology he wrote a number of biblical commentaries while in systematic theology there is a commentary on the *Sentences* and several *summae*.

His knowledge is impressive. None of the Greek, Arab, and Hebrew sources translated in the twelfth and early thirteenth centuries escapes his attention: from the *Guide of Egares* to the commentary of Eustratus on the *Nichomachaean Ethics* and the anonymous *Secret of Secrets*. He placed the intellectual resources of that age at the service of a precise project: to further the scientific inculturation of the *Latini* by offering them a systematic exposition of philosophical and scientific knowledge from the Gentiles. Albert's method of exposition – it is a variation on an "Avicennian style" – assembles a diversity of works to let the texts speak for themselves. He says that one should avoid "reciting the opinions of philosophers without saying anything about whether they are true." His writings can give an impression of eclecticism: for instance, Carl von Prantl (1867) saw him only as a compiler who didn't leave behind his own ideas. This reproach is without foundation. This scholar of Cologne engaged his sources a great deal more than one thinks and takes into account the obscurity of some of them. His thought is remarkably clear.

The reputation of being a "magician" or a "necromancer" has not contributed anything to the balanced interpretation of his thinking. Along with the popularly known *Liber aggregationis seu liber secretorum Alberti Magnis de virtutibus herbarum, lapidum, et animalium quorundam* studying the "power of plants, stones and animals —it sold 227 copies at the Frankfurt book fair of 1569 – many apocryphal works have been attributed to him including the *Secrets of Egyptians*, the most widely circulated book of magic in Germany up to the beginning of the twentieth century, as has *Secrets of Women* (a classic in the genre of exposé). Albert himself is perhaps partly responsible for this exaggerated reputation because he calls himself an "expert in magic" in an unfortunate page of his paraphrase of the *De anima*.[71] This testimony is corroborated by Ulrich of Strasbourg's

---

[71] *De anima* I, 2, 6.

eulogy. "My teacher, Master Albert, at one time bishop of Regensburg, a man divine in every science, the wonder of our time and seen as a wonder, and even educated in magic."[72] What is certain (whether he was or was not "*in magicis expertus*") is that he had read the *Liber prestigiorum of Thabit ibn Qurra* and the *Picatrix* of Ghayat al-Hakim both translated by Adelard of Bath. In the thirteenth century Albert (along with Roger Bacon) was the person who showed the greatest mastery in those sciences and arts that were not taught at the universities. There is astrology/astronomy and particularly alchemy. In the first area his lectures are impressive. He knew at first hand Pseudo-Avicenna's *De caelo et mundo*, Pseudo-Aristotle's *De mansionibus lunace*, and Masallah's *De conjunctionibus planetarum* and the *Interrogationibus*; he had studied the *De imaginibus motus 8e spere* of Thabit ibn Qureran and of course the corpus of Ptolemy completed by the writings of al-Fargani, al-Bitruji, and Maimonides. His contribution to "alchemy" is concentrated in two books edited between 1250 and 1254; it reveals his erudition as it cites along with works of Aristotle and Avicenna further writings attributed to Avicenna and Khalid ibn Yzid, and many texts drawn from Razi and Pseudo-Aristotle.[73]

The extensive presence of Pseudo-Aristotelian writings in the "library" of Albert explains the unusual and original character of his Aristotelianism. There is an influence of "Arab" philosophers, particularly of al-Farabi, Avicenna, and Averroes. Albertinian peripatetic thinking is a totally peripatetic thinking, something built up over time consciously joining as far as possible the rich tradition of interpretations of Aristotle to a basic *factual* ignorance of the history of philosophy and to an absence of philological interests in the modern sense of the term. Interested by the reconstruction of "positions" more than by historical and philological precision, Albert worked to introduce an ordering of ideas and arguments into a corpus of writings whose relationships and chronology he did not know. His philosophical project is coherent and precise in the linear direction of his perspective. We see this in corrections made by him in a manuscript of his own text, "a mature witness to doctrinal struggles of

---

[72] Ulrich of Strasbourg, *De summo bono* IV, 3, 9.

[73] *Mineralia* I, 1, 3.

the thirteenth century."[74] M-Th. D'Alverny in 1929 wrote that at Albert's time there existed at the University of Paris "the expression in Arab thinkers of a liberation with regards to the body, a speculative life, and an acquisition of a supreme happiness by the human person." That project, inspired by al-Farabi and even more by Averroes, guides the thought and interpretation of Albert along perilous paths to where, at the summit, one meets the deifying union according to Christian theology and its "conjunction" with the separated intellect prized by the peripatetics. Again it is al-Farabi who suggested to the teacher of Cologne the theme of "the other life," an *alia vita* that designates "true happiness here on earth." This is a life in philosophy drawing on the language of the masters in arts at Paris in the 1260s whose writings nourish every "Averroism" from the thirteenth to the sixteenth centuries. Simultaneously Albert offered a pattern ascending towards union as he described stages and successive conditions. All this he made the object of his *De intellectu et intellecto* whose hidden matrix is crypto-Plotinian. He too furnished to his student Thomas and the entire age the initial formula of a program of the spiritualization of the human being by a philosophical ascesis as we see in the *Liber exercitationis ad viam felicitatis*.[75] D'Alverny describes its profoundly soteriological dimension. There is a "philosophical" salvation acquired by science and by the practice of virtues in a "community of virtue" which has as its goal removing the soul from corporeal attachments. This is a "supreme happiness of the purest intellectual order, consisting essentially in the contemplation of speculative sciences."

Albert is a militant philosopher. He remains, however, no less a theologian of the Order of Preachers who compels himself to think along the lines of a delicate equilibrium between philosophy and theology. If the problem of a conjunction of natural mysticism and philosophical discipline, gifts of an Arab Aristotelianism, occupies *all* the arts professors in the 1240s to 1265, the question which Albert posed and resolved after 1250 (no longer in Paris but in Germany) met clearly the interests of a subsequent generation or two of teachers in Paris for whom the concordism of al-Farabi and Avicenna was no longer sufficient. In Paris "Averroists" like Siger de Brabant and

---

[74] Paris, Bibliothèque National, Latin ms., 6286.

[75] Edited in 1940 by H. Salman.

Boethius of Dacia along with all the teachers engaged in epistemological reflection study the respective limits of philosophy and theology as sciences, their areas of competence, their principles and methods, and their degrees of certitude in theory. To this issue – not the *unicity of truth* but rather *the unicity of knowing* – Albert contributed a great deal. One can even say that he played there a particularly important role in the acclimatization and legitimation of the life of philosophy at the University of Paris. He affirmed the irreducibility of the two sciences, "distinct in their principles," theology "based on revelation and prophecy" and philosophy "based on reason."[76] Reasoning stands behind the autonomy of philosophical research ("I don't come across God's miracles when I research nature"[77]). Furthermore, he criticized "the preachers" (preachers at the University and not the Friars Preachers) who in their sermons "attack by every means the employment of philosophy without letting anyone respond to them."[78]

Albert did not argue for a doctrine of double truth. He looked for a strict determination of the proper object of each science whether that be philosophy or theology. As he conceived it, theology is not in competition with first philosophy nor is it the school master for the natural sciences. It belongs to the philosopher to speak about the things of nature while it is proper for the theologians to elaborate on the content of revelation in the horizon of a "divine science" essentially nourished by the Dionysian corpus (the *Divine Names* and *Mystical Theology*). In fact, theology in Albert's view only realizes itself in a contemplation by a kind of non-seeing and non-knowing as described in the *Mystical Theology*. There is "a kind of vision in the journey of life" of the philosopher which is mentioned in the commentary on Aristotle's *Ethics*.[79] The duality in virtue of what is infused and what is acquired, the contemplation of God at the end of a demonstration and

---

[76] *Metaphysics* XI, 3, 7.

[77] *De generatione et corruptione* I, 1, 22.

[78] *Commentary on Letter VII of Pseudo-Denys.*

[79] *Super Ethica* X, 16.

the contemplation of God as transcending reason and intellect hold here accurate meanings. This occurs not in the opposition of the teacher of liberal arts to the teacher of theology at the universities but in the dialectic between the philosopher and the mystic. One knows that in the university the teachers of theology did not have to comment on Pseudo-Denys to become a professor. Albert, however, did comment on him. That was part of approaching by meditation true theology. Those works described and supported a clarified object and goal of theological effort even as they expressed the form of the life of the theologian. The subsequent inclusion of the Dionysian body of writings in the library of the theologians, at the summit of a pyramid of writings, is a silent revolution accomplished by Albert whose successors in Germany (the "Rhenish mystics") will harvest the results in Strassburg and Cologne.

The prototype of the theologian according to Albert is not the bishop of Paris Étienne Tempier (the source of the condemnations in Paris of philosophy in 1277) nor is it even Moses. It is the one who contemplates by not knowing and not seeing (*ignorare* and *non-videre*). It is the one who pays attention not to aspects of the object (*rationes subjectae)* but to the unity of which Pseudo-Denys speaks. In short, it is the one whom today we call a "mystic." His name is Hierotheus. The entirety of Albert 's theology finds meaning by reference to a unitive, ineffable experience, the "gift of wisdom" of which (to use the language of Pseudo-Denys) had been granted to a teacher. This experience really is "admirable" in the sense that theology is a *scientia mirabilis.* Theology is the fruit or the heart of a "higher admiration, one higher than the capacity of us to admire." It exists in terms of a *mystical theology* or in terms of a *theology accomplished in unitive contemplation.* Albert presented a tension between the philosopher and the theologian but not as a tension within theology itself. This individuality in Albert's theological activity, which includes a certain prudence in terms of university theology, is one explanation for the variety of influences that will be active later from the thirteenth to the fifteenth centuries.

Joachim R. Söder

Albert the Great, 'The Astonishing Wonder'

"My teacher, Albert, at one time the Bishop of Regensburg, was in every science an almost divine person, so much so that he can be described as the astonishing wonder of our time." Pride is evident in those words of Ulrich of Strassburg as he recognized that he had received his decisive intellectual formation from one of the great figures of an age. Even Roger Bacon, Albert's sharp critic and competitor, admits. "Actually, I praise him more than all other scholars, because he is to the highest degree a man intent upon study." Who is this *doctor universalis*, this person whom the ages after him called "the Great"?

Albert of Lauingen, born shortly before 1200, came from a knightly family in Swabia. As a young man he attended the University of Padua and learned there the new spirituality of the mendicant orders. Most likely, at Easter, 1223, that son of an affluent family entered the community of the Friars Preachers. Where Albert made his novitiate and his theological studies is not known: there are arguments that it would have been Cologne. In the 1230s we find him already serving as the lector (the director of studies) in various German priories like Hildesheim, Regensburg, and Strassburg. Around the age of forty he was sent by his superiors to the University of Paris, the intellectual center of Europe, to attain the doctorate in theology and to assume a professorship there.

Universal Scholar and a Man of Action

The writings in systematic theology which Albert composed in Paris indicate that at that time he already had a detailed knowledge of the church fathers, Aristotle, and Arab thinkers. He planned large projects for research: a "*Summa* on the Entire Reality of Creation" and a commentary on all the writings of Dionysius Areopagita. An intellectual plan is emerging which would fashion an encompassing system of knowledge including and preserving the proper identities of natural science, philosophy, and theology. Then in Paris, a gifted, twenty year old student comes to Albert, someone who will eventually exceed his teacher: Thomas Aquinas. With him as his assistant Albert in 1248 went to Cologne to begin a house of studies for his Order after the model of Paris, an institution that became the first school in the format of a university in Germany and is the precursor of the University of Cologne. Most likely both Dominicans were present at the laying of the corner stone for the new Cologne cathedral being built in the Gothic style.

Albert in Cologne labored over an examination of the new approach to science: he would comment extensively on all the works of Aristotle (and on some of those not written by Aristotle). Behind this project is the insight that in the *corpus Aristotelicum* a system of science is present allowing the real world to be described in a balanced way under the conditions of its creaturely characteristics. So between 1250 and 1270 about forty commentaries and paraphrases -- some of them are lengthy -- on all the known texts of Aristotle were written. They were expanded by Albert's own compositions and by commentaries on other sources, texts the scholar used to fill in what he suspected were "missing pieces" in the Aristotelian corpus and system. Tirelessly the passionate researcher worked on his project even when he had to take on offices like that of provincial of the German Dominican province from 1254-1257 which required that he travel through an area reaching from Bruges to Riga. As a member of the delegation defending the mendicant orders before the Pope, he gave lectures to the *Curia Romana*. In 1260, against the protest of the Master of the Dominican Order, Humbert of Romans, he became bishop of Regensburg (this gave him the rank of a prince in the German *Reich*), but after a year or so he resigned. Further months were spent at the papal court before he returned to Germany: first, as a preacher of a new crusade; then in 1260 as a teacher at the Dominican priory in Würzburg where his brother Heinrich lived and subsequently as a teacher in Strassburg. He returned in 1269 to Cologne. In those years of frequent change Albert wrote large commentaries on books of the Bible: on the Gospels, the prophets, and Job.

Undeterred by his official obligations, the Dominican was much engaged in pastoral work: he preached, and as a bishop he dedicated churches and altars. He served as a mediator amid civic turmoil, being involved in about twenty disputes as "the advocate of peace." The most important of these were two severe conflicts between the Archbishop and citizens of Cologne.

As he worked on the second part of his *Summa theologiae* – the work remained incomplete -- the theologian Albert was taking up the project of a systematic overview of "the wonderful science of God." Albert died on November 15, 1280 in Cologne. When the old Dominican church of Holy Cross was destroyed under Napoleon his grave was moved to where it is today, in the church of St. Andreas.

Unity in Diversity

Albert's life, thought, and activity bear the marks of a drive to what was large, to what was great. Perhaps the medieval idea of the university as an encompassing unity for the various sciences had made a deep impression in the teaching of the *doctor universalis*. The great achievement of the man from Lauingen, one that has survived the centuries, is to meet the challenges posited by a purely inner worldly, reason-oriented, and secular explanation for the world. This is present in the philosophy of Aristotle against which there was occasionally bitter theological resistance. He wanted to show that the Christian religion of revelation, accepted in conviction by faith can be brought together with science. That union of philosophy and theology became paradigmatic, fashioning for centuries the spiritual terrain of Europe. Moreover, through this turn the heritage of antiquity in the Latin cultural area again became vital and fruitful. Albert's "system," pointing to the proper areas of natural science, philosophy and theology, brought him two honorary titles: patron of the natural sciences and of doctor of the church.

Cardinal Karl Lehmann

Albert the Great's Conception of Theology

I

It is well known that Christianity fashioned in a particular way the idea of theology. Scripture in the format of the Bible is the decisive foundation for faith and for theology. The Second Vatican Council says: "Sacred theology relies on the written Word of God taken together with sacred Tradition, as on a permanent foundation. By this Word it is most firmly strengthened and constantly rejuvenated, as it searches out, under the light of faith, the full truth stored up in the mystery of Christ."[1]

And yet Christianity is not a religion of books. The word of God in Scripture reaches out beyond its own languages to other cultural, historical, and social realms. Moreover, each believer should give an account of his or her service to the faith and should present to people reasons for the hope active within them. Theology, therefore, is an "account of hope" (1 Peter 3:15), something that belongs in a basic way to the life of a conscious and personally engaged Christian. Because Christian faith from the beginning includes a public explanation and proclamation of the Gospel, reflection on Christian faith emerged very early. In contrast to other religions Christianity developed and pursued the rational format of theology as it is known today. "That phenomenon which assumes in the High Middle Ages through the form of methodological reflection the term 'Theology' but which in a basic way is found in other forms too is present *only in Christianity*. This characteristic and historical fact should not then be reduced to a general area of theology amid the history of religions. A central sign of this development is that faith on its own moves towards understanding in a suitable way within a contextual mode of understanding"[2] Christian faith itself gives the reason why theology is possible and even necessary. Unavoidably faith in its movement into theology has been fashioned by different conceptions of knowing. Without a doubt the history of science and the theory of knowledge

---

[1] Vatican II, *Dei Verbum* 24.

[2] Gerhard Ebeling, "Theologie," *Religion in Geschichte und Gegenwart* VI (Tubingen: Mohr Siebeck, 1962) 759-61.

have influenced theology and have themselves been co-formed by theology up into modern times.

We see at once a problem prominent in the history of theology: the relationship between *"auctoritas"* and *"ratio,"* "authority" and "reason." That duality has for a long time implied a general rule that all knowing must have a beginning, that knowing takes over the intellectual heritage of the past and relates to it, and that knowing has in itself the task and obligation to develop and further fashion this heritage. *"Auctoritas"* is a truth which is offered as authoritatively guarded and protected through tradition; it needs *"ratio"* to grasp its real content and to unfold its inner import. The brief phrase *"fides quaerens intellectum"* is well known; early on and into the central period of scholasticism those words indicated the task of theology. [3] Later this formula had a more limited meaning, and came to mean the problem of how the claim of revelation could be justified before reason.

II

There is no doubt that theology was designated very early on as science (obviously "science" here was a relatively general idea including a large number of approaches and methods, and a great deal of what was called science included little self-examination). This theology, presented as a science, employs concepts and methods used in other sciences. Every new step in the progress of the general development of science led theology further.

In the twelfth century basic changes occured.[4] Knowledge of the works of Aristotle brought a radical challenge. This is true first in terms of the logical writings of Aristotle but later also in light of his *Ethics* and *Metaphysics*. Those writings led to serious conflicts between philosophers and theologians because the theologians saw themselves drawn to the commentaries of pagan, Jewish, and Muslim scholars whose world-views were radically different from those of Latin Christianity. "The traditional method of theologians had been to show an agreement between different opinions, for instance between Bede

---

[3] See A. Lang, *Die Entfaltung des apologetischen Problems in der Scholastik des Mittelalters* (Freiburg: Herder, 1962) 16-26.

[4] See M.-D. Chenu, *La théologie au douzième siècle* (Paris: J. Vrin, 1966).

and Augustine. This procedure as it was developed in the twelfth century had the goal of eliminating differences among the Latin fathers of the church. It met serious difficulties, however, when one tried to harmonize the Platonic idea of a world-soul with Christian teaching."[5] Naturally there was also an educated opposition. "Forces arose from various camps arguing against the development of theology beyond simply the study of the Bible, and against the systematization of the material and the refinement of a rigorous method. Nonetheless, the basic polemic against scientific theology did not succeed. Its opponents achieved only the condemnation of the content of particular propositions or texts."[6]

Albert the Great quickly recognized the significance of the tension with pagan philosophy and addressed with all his powers controversial areas like the eternity of the world, the unity of the intellect, and the autarchy of the philosophical form of life. It was possible to adjudicate claims for truth and validity standing in opposition to each other if one was ready to explain the reasons for the disagreement from the perspective of a philosophizing reason.[7]

The new place for this enterprise is the emerging theological faculty at the university. Theology has become its partner in dialogue, for the faculty of theology with its own identity employed to a certain degree a similar rational method. Albert the Great in his commentary on a letter of Dionysius Areopagita criticized some of his Dominican brothers because they fought against philosophy and blasphemed about important matters which they did not at all understand.[8] Albert did not permit himself to be seduced into thinking that Aristotle and

---

[5] C. Lohr, "Theologie und/als Wissenschaft im frühen 13. Jahrhundert," *Communio* 10 (1981): 318.

[6] U. Köpf, *Die Anfänge der theologischen Wissenschaftstheorie im 13. Jahrhundert* (Tubingen: Mohr, 1974) 38.

[7] See Ludger Honnefelder, "Albertus Magnus und die Aktualität der mittelalterlichen Philosophie," in Ludger Honnefelder and M. Dryer, eds., *Albertus Magnus und die Editio Coloniensis* (Munster: Aschendorff, 1999) 27.

[8] See M. Burger, "Das Verhältnis von Philosophie und Theologie in den Dionysius-Kommentoren Alberts des Grossen," in J. A. Aertsen and A. Speer, eds., *Was ist Philosophie im Mittelalter?* (Berlin: de Gruyter, 1998) 579-86.

his pagan commentators are new idols. His saying is well known: "Whoever believes that Aristotle was a god must presume that he never errs; who takes him for a human being has no doubt that he can err just as we can."[9] In questions about the Christian faith Albert would believe Augustine before Aristotle; in a philosophy of nature he would prefer Aristotle. A phrase Albert used in a strict methodological conclusion drew from this point of view: in the philosophy of nature miracles do not interest him.[10]

A new model of the relationship between philosophy and theology was needed. Both are independent disciplines. One can realistically relate them when one has made room for the suitable independence of each. They have different ways of knowing. "Knowing can be of two kinds. One form refers to all that is accessible to the knowledge of reason, and that kind is cultivated adequately through research and teaching. Another kind concerns knowledge which our reason does not reach. Knowledge of this sort, of a high nature, needs participation in the fullness of light."[11] Theology is concerned with the content of faith. At its center are the articles of faith in the creed with their presuppositions and consequences. These are the principles of faith, and through them theology is drawn forth out of the light of revelation.

III

Albert's basic model needs a full presentation, although this is not necessary for researchers who have themselves contributed much towards an understanding of it. Briefly I will sketch the interesting conviction of Albert that theology is an "affective science."

We need first to look at some important presuppositions.[12] Today's readers must recall that faith like knowledge is not being described as a purely personal activity. Rather, a system of propositions from faith belongs to faith while to knowing belongs the connection of proofs

---

[9] Albertus Magnus, *Physics* 1, 8 tr 1, c. 14

[10] Honnefelder, "Albertus Magnus," 29.

[11] Albertus Magnus, *Super Dionysii De divinis nominibus* c. 3.

[12] See the introduction to Ingrid Craemer-Ruegenberg, *Albertus Magnus* in the new edition of 2005.

with each scientific discipline."[13] We should notice the kind of objects involved. Despite similar issues, particularly in areas of metaphysics (mainly that of Aristotle), there are considerable differences between philosophy and theology. Theoretical sciences presuppose their fields of inquiry while theology seeks, finds, and makes known its own realm, God. Walter Senner summarizes what is basic in Albert's thought: "The object of theology is, in a quite general way, realities and signs (an old formulation of theology—*res et signa*) that refer to salvation. A particular object is what is to be believed; theology's object in the most precise and highest sense is God as the origin and goal of all beings."[14]

An important question touches the unity of theology as a discipline. Does theology belong to the theoretical or practical sciences? Albert's answer is that theology is neither exclusively theoretical nor practical.[15] He shows here considerable independence in reference to the impact of Aristotle. Theology is not a "science" in the ordinary meaning of the word, not a science about God. It is, first of all, a teaching through which men and women are led to God as the origin of the world and the goal of all their activity and striving. In theology it is not a question of just knowing all that is knowable nor even establishing a theology concerned with the means needed to reach a goal of rational activity. Theology has to do with salvation. Still, Albert does not overlook how important is truth as he emphasizes that practical philosophy has to do with something being done. "The solution is found in the fact that the idea of the truth (*verum*) can be unfolded in two ways. It can be seen as the goal of the speculative understanding of the human being: there truth has a relationship to

---

[13] Craemer-Ruegenberg, *Albertus Magnus* 52.

[14] W. Senner, "Zur Wissenschaftstheorie der Theologie im Sentenzen-Kommentar Alberts des Grossen," in G. Meyer and A. Zimmermann, eds., *Albertus Magnus-Doctor Universalis (1280-1980)* (Mainz: Matthias-Grünewald, 1980) 323-43.

[15] For these basic issues see M. Burger, "Die Bedeutung der Aristotelesrezeption für das Verständnis der Theologie als Wissenschaft bei Albertus Magnus," in Ludger Honnefelder, et al., eds., *Albertus Magnus und die Anfänge der Aristoteles-Rezeption im lateinischen Mittelalter* (Münster: Aschendorff, 2005) 281-305.

what is known by the knowing intellect and consist in its full conceptual content. On the other hand, there is the idea of the true not as something knowable but as something making one happy: '*Verum beatificans intellectum.*' This fulfilling truth lies not in the understanding of the human person alone but comes to a human person. It is not a merely logical relationship but is the highest goal – and is the light radiating out from that goal animating the intellect as it encounters that light. This first truth is sought by the believer for its own sake and not because it holds something worth striving for. Therefore faith does not relate to truth only in the mode of seeking what is good, for then the first truth would no longer itself be the goal. The human achievement of knowing – in the act of faith it consists in agreeing with the content of faith -- is brought into play through the light of the first truth which recalls the simple light of knowing."[16]

Albert determined the epistemological goal of theology to be "*veritas quae secundum pietatem est.*"[17] This allows him to distinguish two aspects in it. On the one hand, there is the goal to which the search for this truth is directed; on the other hand, there is all that ordered to it: the exercise of devotion to God. So Albert called theology a "*scientia affectiva*" in which the theological aspect and the practical dimension are united in a transcendent way. Although "*affectus*" and "*intellectus*" designate different realms of the soul, willing and knowing, Albert was speaking precisely with his phrase "*intellectus affectivus.*" He wanted to integrate the "*affectus*' and its highest goal, God as love, into potentialities of the human person as a knower. Affective knowing brings the intellectual and affective powers to a higher form.[18] What is in play is a principle – and more than a principle – of a thinking concerned with means and reasons. In the total and unified activity of the human person not just mental speculation but the feelings of the human person ("*intellectus extenditur in affectum*") are in play. A firm decision in a free acceptance influences faith. Understanding and will merge. So theology stands beyond the difference of "theoretical" and "practical." Theology is a piety reaching beyond intellectual knowledge.

---

[16] W. Senner, "Zur Wissenschaftstheorie der Theologie," 335f.

[17] Albert, *I Sent.*, d. 1, a. 4, sol.

[18] *Ibid.*

Here it is evident how much Albert stands in the luminous circle of St. Augustine and other numerous predecessors. He also thinks out of a theology drawn from the metaphor of light, one in close connection to Neo-Platonism. So, precisely at the center of a teaching about theology as *"scientia affectiva"* the considerable influence of Aristotle and his Arabic commentaries is limited by a powerful strain of Platonic and Platonic-Augustinian thinking. Consequently a description like "Christian Aristotelianism" does not do justice to the truly synthetic power of Albert the Great. He is always capable, even in an Aristotelian system of sciences, to consider and employ other strands. M. Burger writes: "Summing up, we can conclude that the reception of Aristotelian works influenced in various ways the understanding of theology as a science with Albertus Magnus. The understanding of science present in the *Analytica posteriora* is the first standard by which every claim to science is to be measured. The criteria presented there are now drawn in to develop theology in the form of questions. A strict application, however, is not suitable to the special character of theology as his consequent treatment of *principia* and *habitus* show...Moreover, this practical direction is not to be identified with ethics, for it is found not in the perfection of the virtues nor in a worldly *felicitas* but in a loving reception of the first truth in which uncreated *beatitudo* is the goal."[19]

Albert modifies the Aristotelian understanding of science so much that one can ask whether science in a pure mode is still being discussed. "The problematic emerges out of an Aristotelian perspective. When we begin by observing that Albert has correctly understood Aristotle and is still able to affirm that theology is a science, the apparent contradiction can be resolved if we assume the perspective of Albert the theologian. As a theologian Albert need not do justice to the essentially Aristotelian point of view. He does not need to force theology into the straitjacket of a system which is foreign to theology. Rather, he lets Aristotle stimulate forms in theology and give a foundation for the development of theology. Theology is not being reformulated by a foreign thinking but the perduring content of Christian theology seeks to understand itself anew. In general, the meeting with Aristotelian philosophy leads to a new understanding of what theology can be and receives new accents for treating particular

---

[19] Burger, "Die Bedeutung" 301.

theological themes. The encounter with pagan philosophy stimulates Christian theology. Albert is not inclined to describe himself as an Aristotelian theologian. He uses Aristotle where it seems suitable without neglecting the Neo-Platonic way of thinking which certainly stands closer to Christian thought."[20]

Here in an independent way Aristotelian, Platonic, and Augustinian currents flow together. It has always been rightly observed that with Albert a number of motifs and forms lie next to each other without being merged; in fact, he does not always adequately integrate them. Still, these reflections have their value, for we are gaining a glimpse into the process of his thinking, into his laboratory of theology.

St. Albert's ideas are nourished by a strong spiritual dynamic. As far as I can see, no large school of followers takes up the thought of Albert after him, although it is strongly present in his student Ulrich von Strassburg and later in Giles of Rome.[21] And too, it seems that later in life Albert himself in a theological *Summa* appropriated a rather Franciscan view according to which the truth of theology is first shown in external works and virtues.[22] Those ideas of Albert were somewhat set aside by Thomas Aquinas as he developed a concept of theology marked by strict logic. Certainly Thomas considerably weakened Albert's theory with his view that theology is a *"scientia subalternata."*[23]

IV

From today's point of view Albert's approach is burdened by its concepts and words. It is difficult to translate the verbal set of words coming from "affect" and "affective; indeed, it is hard to translate the Latin *"affectus"* adequately. In general, words coming from "feel" help, although "feeling" in modern times has a strong psychological and subjective accent so that its employment for understanding what we have just presented is not easy. "Feeling" has become the polar opposite to reason -- and this development has a long history. Already

---

[20] Ibid. 301-03.

[21] See U. Köpf, *Die Anfänge* 201-222.

[22] Ibid. 202, 204.

[23] See U. Köpf 145-54; 168-173; 239-44.

in ancient thought pathos (the best Greek equivalent to *"affectus"*) has a broad spectrum of meanings, a spectrum whose limits remain unclear. Moreover, in the teaching in the Stoa about affections the meaning of *"pathos"* and *"affectus"* is drawn off into activity in the senses, something quite different. No doubt there are later attempts to free affectivity and to give it a broader meaning: we find initiatives in this direction, for instance, in the teaching of Thomas Aquinas on the emotions.[24]

Recent attempts in this area are not completely satisfactory. [25] Studies transposing and transforming the content of "pathos" and "affectus" in recent philosophies – for instance, with Martin Heidegger,[26] O. F. Bollnow,[27] and Erich Bloch[28] – have not really succeeded. The writings of Max Scheler only increased the problems of the discussion.[29] A study by Paola-Ludovica Coriando is useful.[30] Under various headings and themes it presents attempts by thinkers to avoid a conflict between "affect" and "feeling," something that happens, for instance, in the idea of the heart according to Blaise Pascal.[31] Poetry too can contribute to understanding affectivity[32] as indicated in some new reflections from Ernst Tugendhat.[33]

---

[24] See J. Lanz, H. Herring, "Affekt," *Historisches Wörterbuch der Philosophie* I (Basel: Schwabe, 1971) 89-101; see the articles in *Theologische Realenzyklopädie* and *Wörterbuch der phänomenologischen Begriffe*.

[25] Ingrid Cramer-Ruegenberg, ed., *Pathos, Affekt, Gefühl*: philo-sophische Beiträge (Freiburg: Alber, 1981).

[26] Heidegger, *Sein und Zeit* (Frankfurt: Klostermann, 1977) 178-86.

[27] *Bollnow, Das Wesen der Stimmungen (Frankfurt: Klostermann, 1956).*

[28] Bloch, *Das Prinzip Hoffnung* (Frankfurt: Francke, 1959).

[29] Scheler, *Wesen und Formen der Sympathie* (Bern: Suhrkamp, 1973).

[30] Coriando, *Affektenlehre und Phänomenologie der Stimmungen. Wege einer Ontologie und Ethik des aemotionalen* (Frankfurt: Klostermann, 2002).

[31] Ibid. 26-29.

[32] Ibid. 157-232.

[33] Tugendhat, *Egozentrizität und Mystik* (Munich: Beck, 2003).

Theology in its history of forms did not stand still in this area. Again and again there is a move away from an exaggerated intellectualism. The basic direction of Augustinian-Franciscan thought has always protected itself from that one-sidedness. Other directions and principles could be drawn into an understanding of theology as elements of an "affective theology" like apophatic theology and mystagogical theology. There are always requests for a praying theology, a theology on the knees, for attempts to draw from affectivity theologies of preaching aimed at the emotions.

At any rate, those basic ideas of St. Albert the Great need not be absent from today's enterprise of theology. His contribution is of value in two ways. First, there is the experience that the "object" of theology, God himself, again and again enters the lives of men and women. God comes to a person and touches her. This phenomenon of coming to the person cannot be absent. Second, it is clear that in the realm of God one can only approach God with suitable ways of thinking, with suitable thought-forms. The Most High must be understood through the highest powers of knowing. These are contained in the idea of an "affective science." Here we have a certain proximity to the phenomenology of the holy. Husserl's knowledge of the corre-spondence of noesis and noema is also important. We come near to a primal meaning of "pathos" when we ponder an encounter or impact that is total, intellectual and born by ourselves. To describe what is meant by this in a contemporary understanding of words drawn from "feeling" is hardly adequate. Albertus Magnus urges us to pursue in a new way these concepts somewhat lost in the distant past.

I am convinced that faith needs thinking if it is to remain true to itself. Faith in its role of illumining the world and giving meaning to human existence is irreplaceable and cannot be absorbed by an utterly self-contained knowing. Still, what is "theology"? Is not faith alone adequate? Further, will faith in its special reality and value be endangered precisely if it is analyzed and taken over by human sciences? Can faith remain faith when science concerns itself with faith? These are serious questions and have occupied theology in various ways from its beginnings up to today.[34]

---

[34] See B. Langenohl, ed., *Wozu Theologie?* (Münster: Lit, 2005).

We recall the Pauline word about the Christian message as the foolishness of the cross, "a stumbling block to the Jews and folly to Gentiles" (1 Cor. 1:23). One thinks back to the struggles with pagan philosophies, struggles between faith and knowing. The phrase, "reason the prostitute," comes not only from Luther but from Bonaventure. Varied answers have been given to this topic. Again and again, up to the theology of Karl Barth, there has been the opinion that theology emerges because one needs it as a defense against heresies, as a protection of the faith against mis-interpretations. This thesis -- the need for theology comes mainly from the reality of heresies – does find some examples in church history. "It is necessary there be heresies "(1 Cor 11:19). Paul's words suggest a constant struggle. Whatever the answers is, it appears that the thesis of the birth of theology from the fact of heresies presents perhaps a "historical" but only a quite partial truth. It hardly answers adequately the question, "Why is there a faith that thinks, a theology?" To conclude, I would repeat my conviction: faith needs thinking if faith is to be true to itself.

Ulrich Horst, O.P.

Albertus Magnus and Thomas Aquinas as Commentators on *The Gospel according to Matthew 16:18.* A Contribution to the Teaching on Papal Primacy

Albert wrote a commentary on the *Gospel according to Matthew*, his *Super Mathaeum,* in the years between 1257 and 1264.[1] The scope of the work is striking. Just the topics considered there in commenting on the sixteenth chapter of the Gospel – the chapter concerning the topic of this essay, the words of Jesus to Peter – are extensive. Albert's commentaries on the other Gospels, particularly on Luke, are also of an impressive size. Possibly their length has hindered more than encouraged an adequate evaluation of their exegetical method and theology. The following essay aims at making a small contribution towards understanding Albert's exegetical theology as it ponders a text important for Albert's own perspective. Then it turns to the exegesis of his student Thomas Aquinas. Finally there is a comparison of their conclusions. Ideas on papal primacy as the two Dominicans present them in other writings will be used only occasionally to illustrate a particular point. Because the biblical text here is quite significant and full of implications, it is legitimate to suspect that the doctrine and theology found in its exegesis gives typical ideas, typical also because the authors comment on this pericope from presuppositions common to both. We will look particularly at the sources and conclusions they draw from the Scriptures and from the Fathers of the church. Even if Albert and Thomas were conscious that they were engaged with a controversial reality, one will have to consider that each will spotlight in different ways the primacy of Peter and the pope.

Thomas, because of his active involvement in the controversy in Paris over the existence of the mendicant orders (his opusculum *Contra impugnantes Dei cultum et religionem* is a result of this) and because of his time in Orvieto involving him in issues touching the union of the Western church with the Greeks and giving him access to

---

[1] Albertus Magnus, *Super Matthaeum.* See also the commentary on *Isaiah* as well as Albert Fries, "Zur Entstehungszeit der Bibel-kommentare Alberts des Grossen," in G. Meyer, A. Zimmermann, eds., *Albertus Magnus Doctor universalis (1280-1980)* (Mainz: Matthias-Grünewald, 1980) 119-39.

further texts from the Greek fathers, had knowledge and interests different from those of Albert in Cologne.[2] A comparison of the two Dominicans presumes differences and distinctions between the two theologians although common characteristics will emerge.

The following examination does not require an analysis of the entire scene at Caesarea Philippi but stays with the verses touching our theme. It is significant that Peter before the others and representative of the others answers the question of the Lord about who the disciples say he is. This role is already grounded in his name "Simon" which means "obedience." Personal merit and suitability for giving the right leadership are also expressed in this name.[3] Obedience to divine commands gives more insight into divine things than serious study could produce.[4] The further name "Peter" was given to him early on (*John* 1:42). From a methodological point of view it is striking that in this area no use of Augustine's commentaries on Petrine texts is made nor any use of St. Jerome's commentary on *Matthew* which Albert knew and used elsewhere. We lack a patristic "treatment" in this section, something to which we will return.

Cephas is translated here with *caput*: the head exercises its proper relationship to and influence on the members of the body. This designates Peter, while the application of *petra* refers to a building with its solid structure. With this process of naming there is expressed why Peter was empowered to answer the Lord's question (who do people say he is), for in Persian Peter means *agnoscens* ("knowing").[5] So in *cephas* there is an allusion to ruling which leads to calling him the head of the Apostles, the pinnacle and head. That permits the

---

[2] Treating Albert's ecclesiology is Wilhelm Scherer, *Des seligen Albertus Magnus Lehre von der Kirche* (Freiburg: Herder, 1928); Walter Principe, "The school theologians' view of the papacy, 1130-1250," in Christopher Ryan, ed., *The Religious Roles of the Papacy. Ideals and Realities 1150-1300* (Toronto: Pontifical Institute of Medieval Studies, 1989) 45-116.

[3] Albert, *Super Matthaeum* c. 16, 16

[4] Ibid.

[5] "And in this response we touch on an intellectual faculty, because Peter in Persian means 'one knowing'" (Ibid); see Yves Congar, "Cephas-céphalè-caput," *Revue du moyen-âge latin* 8 (1952): 5-42.

conclusion that he had an ability to recognize what was correct that he would give truth recognized the stability of a rock.[6] On earlier occasions Albert emphasized that Peter was the *vertex apostolorum,* the central point of the Apostles, a designation which emerges from the fact that Peter is first in dignity.[7]

We can pass over the exegesis of the verses leading to the designation of being a rock. Albert discusses presuppositions and the essence of the confession but without presenting further ecclesiological material. With other interpreters Albert saw in the phrase "*ego dico tibi quia tu es Petrus*" a firmness. Jesus' statement is firm, and its firmness can have several references: the foundation of the church, the founding of the church, and the consequent resistance to powers intent upon the church's collapse.[8] The intrinsic reason for the guarantee lies in the person of him who gives it to Peter: Christ is himself the "transforming truth." His words will not pass away, and so he himself is the real foundation. The Lord empowers Peter in light of his preceding confession by addressing him with the name given earlier to the Apostle (*John* 1:42) and now confirmed.[9] Accordingly the church rests on "this rock" of a "strong and immovable confession." Albert seems not to be familiar with the problematic as it was known to the Middle Ages through Augustine's *Retractiones* (we will look more closely at this later): *petra* means here not Peter but Christ. Some other New Testament texts like *I Corinthians* 3:11 state this clearly.[10]

---

[6] "Leadership flows from Cephas, and so he is called the '*vertex*' of the apostles: a gift in knowing and a solidity in recognizing the truth are found in the rock" (*Super Matt.* 456). In the Gregorian reform Bonizo of Sutri called the Roman Curia *vertex et fundamentum omnium ecclesiarum* (Yves Congar, "Der Platz des Papsttums in der Kirchenfrömmigkeit der Reformer des 11. Jahrhunderts," in J. Daniélou, H. Vorgrimler, eds., *Sentire ecclesiam* [Freiburg: Herder, 1961] 196-217).

[7] Albert, *Super Matt.,* c. 10, 2.

[8] "The firmness of confession implies three things: foundation, the founding of the church in a foundation, and a firmness against undermining forces" (*Super Matthaeum,* 16:18).

[9] Ibid. 460.

[10] Ibid. 460.

What does "my church" mean? It is the holy and apostolic church according to the words of the creed. This statement about the church can be studied under four aspects. The church leads a life of holiness; it has a knowledge of the faith and confesses it; it has an authority in the power of the keys; it has an authority in jurisdiction.

The following characteristic is not easy to interpret. Albert spoke of a *congregationum multitudo* without explaining what the expression means. Is it a number of local churches which the *ecclesia universalis* gathers into itself? And too, he speaks of the church enjoying the *regularum veritas*. This idea despite the mention of rules is not immediately understandable. The observation that heresy cannot attack these rules suggests that legal and doctrinal areas are meant: these are rules giving to the church suitable defenses against all attacks. To the conclusion drawn from this – "in this way the church is Catholic" – Albert added a quotation from Boethius which is so general that a clear meaning is not evident. Finally, the opinion of many theologians at that time, including Dominicans, is that "the gates of hell" are heresies and mortal sins. [11]

It is worth noting that Albert, standing in a long tradition, joined the guarantee that the church remains in the truth not to the person of Peter or to that of his successor but to the entire church. A shift from a statement directed to Peter to a statement directed to the church occurs without contrasting the two. There is no mention here of the *ecclesia Romana* as a source and place of fidelity in the faith. This, however, certainly does not mean that such an idea is foreign to him. Albert applied a text from the *Gospel according to Luke* (22:32), a text with great ecclesiological significance ("I have prayed for you that your faith does not fail") to Peter, and totally in the sense of tradition, to his see. Because Peter is the first apostle, the Lord directed his prayer to him so that through him "this strengthening could flow on to the others." The prayer, however, does not preserve Peter from all vacillations in faith; it preserves him only *finaliter*, "in reference to the end," or during the time between history and its end. In other words, in the future there will be deviations from time to time. And finally, that protection is an "effective argument" for the *sedes Petri*, the *Romana Ecclesia*, and Peter's successors in the see of Rome. This

---

[11] For instance, Hugh of St. Cher and Thomas Aquinas.

means that Albert referred the prayer not primarily to the person of the occupant but to the chair, the diocesan see, the "seat."[12]

What are "the keys of the kingdom of heaven" promised to Peter? The keys are not, as many think, a discerning knowledge and power of binding and losing but rather the authority to distinguish concerning lepers (*Leviticus* 13: 1-45) and a power of judgment concerning sins. Knowledge in the exercise of the keys helps the exercise of the power of the keys, because knowledge and authority do not always coincide in the same person. The power of binding and losing is active in the exercise of judging which certainly finds in knowledge a reasonable enterprise.[13] Has only Peter been raised to the level of having the power of the keys? Albert paid special attention to this question. He had already treated it in three other sections of his commentary dedicated to this topic before he answers it definitively here. Looking at the calling of the first disciples (*Matthew* 4:18) he stated that the administration of the sacraments, teaching, and church ministries have been entrusted to them. In light of the power connected to those activities it is absolutely necessary that in that circle one person will be entrusted with a "general and full power." Helpers (*coadjutores*) would be given to him "in the work of the shepherd's caring ministry" (*in opera sollicitudinis*) because the human person is weak. That means that Peter alone cannot himself fulfill this assigned ministry and so other are called "to participate in it."[14] In writing about the calling of Peter and Andrew, Albert mentioned that no matter how great the dignity and power of a person he needs in many things the help of another. So in the case of Peter to whom a general power is given, although he alone is the head of the church (according to his added name *Cephas* which means head), he cannot alone bear the heavy burden of the duties of ministry. So Andrew is called "to be with

---

[12] *Super Lucam* 685 (on chapter 22:32).

[13] *Super Matthaeum.* on 16, 18; see Ludwig Hödl, *Die Geschichte der scholastischen Literatur und der Theologie der Schlüsselgewalt* I (Münster: Aschendorff, 1960).

[14] "Here the second part begins treating the calling of the ministers through whom the sacraments and teaching are dispensed as well as the offices of the church. In the power of the ministers it is necessary that some have a universal power but they need helpers" (Ibid. 96).

him."[15] Albert made a third comment on our text and topic. Calling Peter the *primus vertex* should not lead one to conclude that Andrew and Phillip are a second and third head. They are all Apostles related to the jurisdiction of Peter; all are "second" because all are ordered to Peter.[16]

This theology helps us understand Albert's exegesis of *Matthew* 16:10. When the Lord uses "you" in his address to Peter he means Peter as one person (*singulariter*). That does not mean that Peter alone received power. The singular indicates that there is one receiving power for a fullness in the organization of the church. The goal of this arrangement is unity. This one is the successor of Peter: in fact, he is Peter in terms of power. That power lives on in each pope for they live in the power that was given to the Apostle who is first. All the others, the bishops, receive that power in the same unity but as participants in this power because they are called into a pastoral co-ministry. If earlier Peter alone was addressed, one must now direct one's attention to the reception of the Holy Spirit (*John* 20:22) by a group in which the power to forgive sins is contained.[17] Albert's teaching about the highest power in the church, presented in relatively few texts, is clear when it is placed in the context of his time. Peter enjoys the *plenitudo potestatis* to which the Apostles are ordered.

This describes the later relationship between pope and bishops. Unity and structural order in the church require this perspective. The Apostles already at the inception of their public activity were called by the Lord to participate in pastoral ministry and to assist Peter in the exercise of his ministry and office. They have an orientation to the see of Peter: a dependence on it results. Nowhere, however, is it said that the proper jurisdiction given to the Apostles and bishops in terms of the *sollicitudo* for the local church is derived in its proper jurisdiction from Peter or from his successors. The fullness of power given to them

---

[15] Ibid. 97.

[16] *Ibid, 320.*

[17] "He uses 'you' in the singular not because he appoints Peter singularly but because in the unity of the order of the church there is one who receives 'fullness of power' and who is the successor of Peter and is Peter in power. In terms of power, others receive in that one unity." (Ibid. 461).

pluraliter to forgive sins comes, much more, immediately from the Lord himself.[18]

Two further texts confirm this interpretation. In his commentary on *John* (20:23), Albert wrote that Peter alone receives the fullness of power, while the others participate in that pastoral ministry.[19] In the *Commentary on the Sentences* he explains (drawing on *Matthew* 16:19 and *Luke* 22:32) that the Lord placed Peter over the others and established a fixed structure for ecclesiastical jurisdiction. That structure is fashioned in such away that the first Apostle gives the exercise of the office to the disciples when Christ breathes on them giving them the Holy Spirit.[20] While Christ himself has given them the ministry, it belonged to Peter to direct the Apostles into concrete ministry and into their own areas of jurisdiction. Today it is the concern of the pope to do this.

Agreeing with this view are statements in *De mysterio missae*. Those who consider this writing to be by Albert receive some support for their view from these passages, for they recall the theology just presented.[21] Through the pope, the father of all fathers, the successor of Peter and vicar of Christ, the community of the church "flows" into others so that the presentation of the offering of the Eucharist is without value if one separates oneself from the unity of the chuches

---

[18] See Kenneth Pennington, *Pope and Bishops: The Papal Monarchy in the Twelfth and Thirteenth Centuries* (Philadelphia: University of Pennsylvania Press, 1984).

[19] "Here he says to all (*John* 20: 23): 'Receive the Holy Spirit'. And so it seems that all receive the power of the keys....Matthew, however, says, 'Only to Peter do I give them.' This is not difficult to explain because only Peter accepts the fullness of power on the part of all the others" (*Super Johannem* (Borgnet ed., vol. 24, 687).

[20] *IV Sent.* D. 17, a. 10. "Peter proposes to all."

[21] Albert Fries in various publications says that these writings on the Eucharist are not from Albert. Hans Jorissen argues with good reasons for Albert as the author; see H-J. Vogels, "Zur Echtheit der eucharistischen Schriften Alberts des Grossen," *Philosophie und Theologie* 53 (1978): 102-19; A. Kolping, "Zur Entstehungeschichte der Messerklärung Alberts des Grossen," *Münchener Theologische Zeitschrift* 9 (1958): 1-16.

coming from the head and from obedience to the head.[22] In short, the idea that the pope is the principle unifying the church is expressed in two other texts. There is a reference to *Matthew* (16:19): the keys are given to one, to Peter, and the fullness of power rests in one and is given to the others through a commission to share the pastoral ministry.[23] A second text is *Luke* 22:32 where it belongs to the successor of Peter to strengthen the entire church. That commission seems to consist not only in remaining in correct teaching but in sustaining the highest church office.[24]

Of course, Albert's view brings with it problems concerning the highest ecclesial teaching office. At the same time, it is striking that he had no particular interest in this topic of papal power. It is enough for him that the pope enjoys a *plenitudo potestatis* whose goal is to keep the local churches unified and in communion with its leaders. That observation stays on the surface of what is a deeper problem. Why did Albert limit himself in this area? He overlooked the controversy between the diocesan clergy and the mendicant orders concerning the rights of each to be active in pastoral ministry and teaching. For some years it had raised consequences for a new ecclesiological treatment of papal primacy.[25] Albert seems not to have noticed the conflicts in Paris around the middle of the thirteenth century over the confirmation of the mendicants as personal groups transcending and working outside diocesan and parochial structures as well as the canonizations of Saints Francis and Dominic which Bonaventure evaluated as acts of a high and consequently irrevocable teaching authority. They had fashioned a new theological situation.[26] His teaching on *plenitudo potestatis* is neither new nor original: canonists of the previous

---

[22] "'Papa', however, means father of fathers: the successor of Peter, vicar of Jesus Christ" (*De mysterio Missae* III 6).

[23] Ibid. III, 6 and 8.

[24] Ibid. III, 8.

[25] See J. Ratzinger, *Das neue Volk Gottes. Entwürfe zur Ek-klesiologkie* (Düsseldorf: Patmos, 1969) 49-71.

[26] See Ulrich Horst's writings on the controversy over poverty and the mendicant orders.

century had developed it in detail.[27] That Albert in important passages took a conservative line is one surprising result of our study, one supported by an adequate number of passages.

Between Albert's view and the theology of Aquinas emerging at the same time there is the remarkable influence of the Order of Preachers whose areas of experience expanded the ecclesiology they had received. That throws new light on the difficulty of the conflict in Paris and on the originality of the positions of Bonaventure and Thomas Aquinas. Hugh of St. Cher's commentary on the *Sentences* gives some insight into the theological discussion at the Dominican community of St. Jacques; papal authority was apparently not a theme that was being developed there. Albert's precise ecclesiological positions are a stage in a progress and initiate theological discussion of these topics and lead to the later views of Thomas Aquinas.

* * *

In terms of theology, the difference between Albert and Thomas does not need to be evaluated here fully. They represent different ecclesiological perspectives. Aquinas (he taught in Cologne for a short time) was drawn into playing an active role in the controversy over the existence of the mendicant orders, a situation Albert entered only after intensive study of material that was apparently new to him. No less significant was the fact that Aquinas in an early period (as the *Contra impugnantes* was written) placed great importance on having the broadest possible patristic and canonistic support, something developed by his confreres at Saint Jacques in Paris. The situation in Orvieto where sources either unknown to him or hardly used by him were accessible helped him base securely a theological reflection upon patristic theologians and ecumenical councils. Among them were important Greek texts touching on controversies over church union. The *Catena Aurea* with its panoply of Greek and Latin theologians seems to confirm the primacy of the bishop of Rome explicitly, and this exemplifies the approach of Aquinas. Knowledge of certain heresies in the ancient church and the response to them of councils showed him that the *Ecclesia Romana* was constantly the firm pole amid doctrinal storms and survived the ages without serious damage. Albert, on the

---

[27] See M. Rios Fernandez, "El primado del romano pontifice en el pensamiento de Huguccio de Pisa decretista," *Compostellanum* 6 - 11 (1961-1966).

other hand, did not have the same historical interests, the same bent for the history of doctrine. Other problems were of deeper concern to him. And too, he did not have the possibility to gain access to ancient sources which at that time were available extensively in Italy.

Hans Jorissen

The Contribution of Albert the Great to the Theological Reception of Aristotle: The Example of Transubstantiation

Aristotle in the Early Writings of Albert

The study of Albert the Great is always a fascinating adventure. Albert in his early writings used and drew into his theological reflection and writings the Aristotelian corpus. He did this on a large scale in comparison with his contemporaries (to mention only beyond the logical writings the *Physics*, the *Metaphysics*, the *De anima*, the *Nicomachean Ethics*, and the *Parva Naturalia*[1]). His reception of Aristotle is clearly led by theological interests.[2] The ways in which the Aristotelian corpus came to Albert definitely needs to be studied more closely. The issue is not the translations used by Albert which were available already at the end of the twelfth century even if they were not widely circulated.[3] Rather, where in that age did the impulses come from for someone to undertake such an unusually intense study?[4] Regardless, Albert himself is the best argument against the view of Bernard Dod that Aristotle in the academic world of Paris up to around the middle of the thirteenth century played no important role.[5] That is certainly not an accurate view of the theological faculty there nor of William of Auxerre (+1231), Phillip the Chancelor (+1236),

---

[1] See the index of the authors cited by Albert in his early works in Albertus Magnus, *Opera Omnia* 26, 358; Henryk Anzulewicz, *De forma resultante in speculo des Albertus Magnus* (Münster: Aschendorff, 1999).

[2] H. Anzulewicz, "Konzeptionen und Perspektiven der Sinneswahrnehmung im System Alberts des Grossen," *Micrologus* 10 (2002): 23-41; D. N. Hasse, *Avicenna's* De anima *in the Latin West*, (London: The Warburg Institute, 2000) 60-90.

[3] B. G. Dod, "Aristoteles latinus," in Norman Krezmann, et al. eds., *The Cambridge History of Later Medieval Philosophy* (Cambridge: Cambridge University Press, 1982) 46-53, 74-79.

[4] See Ludger Honnefelder, et al., eds., *Albertus Magnus und die Anfänge der Aristoteles-Rezeption im lateinischen Mittelalter* (Münster: Aschendorff, 2005).

[5] Dod, "Aristoteles latinus," 53, 69.

William of Auvergne (+1249), Roland of Cremona (+1259), Hugh of St. Cher (+1263), and it is particularly not accurate for Albert.[6]

An Overview of the Development of the Teaching on Transubstantiation

To evaluate better the contribution of Albert to the clarification of the idea of transubstantiation and to the formation of a doctrine on transubstantiation (including philosophical reflection) a brief overview of how that teaching developed is needed.[7] The European teaching on transubstantiation unfolds in a long and complex process which in its beginnings shows a dominantly neo-Platonic real-symbolic perspective yielding to an understanding of reality more and more formed by Aristotle. In that process one can see how theological developments are determined by philosophical presuppositions.

The immediate occasion is the critique of Berengarius of Tours (+1088) on the Eucharistic theology of change offered by Rathram. Berengarius is the first who makes important the ideas of *"materia,"* *"forma"* *"subjectum,"* *"id quod in subjecto est,"* and *"accidens"* in his critique of change in the Eucharist. *"Materia"* is the same as *"subjectum,"* while *"forma"* means the sum of the characteristics that can be grasped by the senses: it is a co-determining principle determining the essence of a thing. The qualities perceived by the senses belong essentially to the substance of a thing. This idea of substance allied to the senses leads consequently to the denial of the real separation of substance and accident and consequently to the denial of the possibility of a Eucharistic change of natures. Evidently Berengarius measured the idea of change by the kinds of change experienced in nature.

An opposite direction forming a teaching on transformation was needed to make clear and to retain the real presence of the Eucharist (denied by Berengarius according to his opponents). It sought to place the mode of presence in the background and to describe this through a

---

[6] See F. Van Steenbeerghen, *Aristotle in the West. The Origins of Latin Aristotelianism* (Louvain: Nauwelaerts, 1955) 114-26.

[7] See publications by H. Jorissen, J. Wohlmuth, Gary Macy, M. Laarmann, and P. J. J. M. Bakker.

new philosophical way of thinking.[8] J. R. Geiselmann saw there a link to an "Ambrosian metabolism" with a strong terminology of change and with a view of the change itself as a transformation touching the essential status of the elements of consecration. Because of Berengarius' criticism of the idea of change, a theology of metabolism is developed in the direction of an ontological explanation of the process of change. Beregarius' main opponents -- Lanfranc (+1089) and particularly Guitmund of Averesa (+ circa 1090) -- express Eucharistic change as a change in substance (*substantialiter transmutari*). In terms of church teaching this is presented at the Roman Synod of 1079 (*substantialiter converti*). The term "*transsubstantiatio*" according to the report of an anonymous student of Robertus Pullus seems to have appeared first around 1140,[9] and the first text using it is from Magister Rolandus around 1155/56. It finds a rapid and general acceptance and is sanctioned at the Fourth Lateran Council through a conciliar decision (one which is not technically definitive and so not a dogma).

The ontological interpretation of transubstantiation depends on the idea of substance philosophically underlying it. Gilbert of Poitier (+1154) affirms the influential theory of a corporeal substratum of matter and a *forma substantialis*: they are the sum and inner reality of all the essential characteristics. Building upon a common approach at the end of the twelfth century but seeking the goal of finding a conceptual delineation of transubstantiation are two opposing viewpoints. Both of them understand Eucharistic change as the transformation of substance: they are different from each other in their understanding of substance itself.

The representative of the first and dominant direction is Peter Cantor (+1197). For him substance in its application to transubstantiation means matter as the bearer of form (*substantia-materia; substantia a substando*). Only the material essential part is changed while the substantial form, that is the essential properties and

---

[8] See Hans Jorissen, "Berengar von Tours," *Lexikon für Theologie und Kirche* 2 (1994) 244-246.

[9] M. Laarmann, "Transubstantiation," *Archiv fur Begriffsgeschichte* 41 (1999): 122.

accidents, remain. Perduring effects like the capability of giving nourishment are seen by him to lie in the *forma substantialis.*

Over against this view is Alan of Lille (+1202) who is the representative of a second direction. He sees transubstantiation as the changing of the totality of the essence (substance) constituted out of matter and form, and so the substance of bread and wine with the accidents remain behind without a subject.

Towards the end of the twelfth century the understanding of transubstantiation within an Aristotelian terminology of substance and form is, nonetheless, far removed from Aristotelian hylomorphism. Further development unfolds within the growing influence of the reception of Aristotle along the lines of Alan while the view of Peter Cantor finds a disciple in the thirteenth century only in Roland of Cremona. Stephan Langton (+1218) seems to be the turning point; his position is given further precision in terms of a positive change of being by Guido of Orchelles (+1225). With him, in contrast to changes in natural accidents (*alteratio*), the accidents remain and the substance of matter and form passes away without being annihilated or being dissolved in the elements. With William of Auxerre and Hugh of St. Cher, the conceptual determination of transubstantiation shows how the influence of the Aristotelian idea of form in the sense of unified and indivisible principles has arrived. Only with Alexander of Hales is the conceptual clarification of transubstantiation as a change in essence complete, and this occurs on the basis, however, of the real distinction between the metaphysical nature and the characteristics of that nature.

The Idea of Transubstantiation according to Albert the Great.

A comparison between Alexander of Hales and Albert the Great makes it clear how much the Dominican worked to attain a speculative penetration and deepening of this idea. Transub-stantiation is the change of the total substance of bread and wine constituted from matter and substantial form (and only the substance) into the substance of the pre-existing body and blood of the risen Lord. So there is one, inseparable, positive process between two positive terms, something being changed into an *esse melius.* The cessation (*desinere esse*) of the *terminus a quo* is not a collapse (*corruptio, cedere in non esse*) or an annihilation (*annihilatio*) but rather the making present of the body and blood of Christ. This is an emergence, a becoming anew, or an arrival on the basis of a local movement. Albert wrote: "In this sacrament there is a change which in a proper sense can be named transubstantiation because it is a kind (of transubstantiation) of the total substance of a reality into the total substance of another reality; that is, it is a change from the total substance of bread and wine into the total substance of the body and blood of Jesus Christ according to substantial form and matter. The entire composite of bread and wine ceases to exist in terms of its substantial elements."[10] The "*operatio transsubstationis*" (or the act of transubstantiation) refers only to the substance of bread and wine"[11] and in no way refers to a "changing" in Christ. Albert explained: "It is the transubstantiation of a totality into the total body without the body of Christ taking on anything new,"[12] and "there is a change of the total substance into the totally pre-existing substance of another."[13] Therefore transubstantiation is not an annihilation but a *mutatio, in multo melius.*[14] "The total essence of bread is not annihilated nor does the substance of the bread pass into the totality of the body of Christ according to matter and form."[15] And where such a transubstantiation occurs, the bread and wine necessarily remain in the same way, receiving nothing into them and still actively present.[16] "That transubstantiation has only terms and not a common subject which is the third reality in physical change."[17] Transubstantiation supposes a point of departure, a being from which something becomes. "Nevertheless, it does not presuppose this as matter which is in its act that from which and in which transubstantiation takes place, for then there would not be a transubstantiation from the total substance but only from one substantial form....There is for this transubstantiation no substratum.

---

[10] *IV Sent.,* d. 11, a. 1 (Borgnet ed., vol. 29, 266f).

[11] Ibid., d.10, a. 10.

[12] Ibid., d. 10, a. 10; d. 20, a. 6, ad quaest.

[13] Ibid., d. 11, a. 7 ad 9.

[14] *De corpore domini,* d. 13, tr 3, c. 1.

[15] *IV Sent.,* d. 10, a. 1, ad 1.

[16] Ibid., d. 11, a. 1, ad 1.

[17] Ibid., ad 6, 1.

"[18] Consequently the idea of transubstantiation signifies "the *terminus a quo* because this is being changed and this is a being which does not fall back into non-being although the change has to do with the total substance."[19]

What is significant is the clarification of the idea of transubstantiation through a hylomorphic understanding of matter and form. *"Materia"* and *"forma substantialis"* are the constitutive principles (*partes essentiales*) of corporeal beings. Transubstantiation refers (as the above texts have made clear) in a strict sense to the composite constituted out of matter and substantial form (the essential totality) of the substance of bread and wine. A clear distinction between substance and the characteristics of an essence (the properties) which follow immediately from the substance (the accidents) is present. The kind of change affecting only the principles constituting the substance is not found in the realm of the experience of nature, and so is not studied by Aristotle (it could not have occurred to him). According to Albert being can be effected only by *"primum agens infinitae virtutis,"*[20] that is, by God. It is worth noting that precisely with the help of Aristotelian conceptuality the idea of transubstantiation finds a clear expression.[21]

The Problem of Accidents without a Subject: Albert's Commentary on the Sentences.

The above reflections raise the *"quaestio gravissima"* (as Albert titled it) of the possibility of an existence of accidents without a subject in the sacrament of the Eucharist. This question bothered Albert a great deal, for all of philosophy seems to stands against it.[22]

---

[18] Ibid.

[19] Ibid., ad 6, 2.

[20] Ibid., d. 10, a. 1, ad 1; d. 11, a. 1, ad 1.

[21] Albert passed over the question of how the *forma panis* is changed into the *forma corporis Christi*; he decisively rejected a proper *forma corporeitatis*....He did discuss the theory of concomitance.

[22] *IV Sent.*, d. 12, a. 16. "Against this are many objections; all of philosophy seems to be against it" (Ibid.)

Albert's project is to make rationally intelligible and capable of expression the possibility of an existence of accidents without a subject; he is not concerned with a rationalist explanation or a removal of the mystery. Albert said that in relationship to the divine mysteries (he mentions here the Eucharist and the Trinity) adequate concepts are absent, for the divine mysteries transcend our consciousness in such a way that we can, in our thinking and speaking, only echo in a "stuttering" fashion (in the words of Gregory the Great): "It must be said without prejudice that in this topic and in the area of the Trinity words are not sufficient to express the manner of divine activity but we echo the lofty things of God to the extent that we can – by stuttering."[23] He rejected any quick summoning up of a divine miracle as the explanation. This, however, avoids the effort to understand through ideas. He argued decisively against the view that reasons cannot be sought to explain the question of accidents in transubstantiation because here everything seems to contradict the principles of reason.[24] To set aside philosophy prematurely by summoning up *divina miracula* would give an easy and quick solution to every problem. "If we want to respond in this way, we would quickly solve every issue by saying that in all of them there is a divine miracle." A biblical passage (*1 Peter* 3:15) does not permit that. "It is too little to say in the teaching of faith that this or that happens through a divine miracle unless we give some reason for this. It is proper to the teacher not to teach something unless there is a suitable reason for it."[25]

In this issue of the accidents Albert offers philosophical arguments against his own position although in the solution of this question he will still follow philosophy to the extent that it is possible: "holding to the faith and not following philosophy except to the extent that faith is retained."[26] He worked for an explanation that is philosophically viable even with the bestowal of a *virtus divina* at work in the

---

[23] Ibid., d. 10, d. 9, obj. 1 et 2; see Gregory the Great, *Moralia* 1, 5, c. 36, n. 66.

[24] Ibid., d. 10, a. 9, ad 1 and 2.

[25] *De corpore domini*, d. 6, tr 2, c. 1; "And so, what I don't understand I do not presume to defend" (*IV Sent.*, d. 13, a. 10, ad quaest.).

[26] *IV Sent* d. 12, a. 16, sol.

sacrament. Albert arranged three kinds of opposing arguments: 1) the "definition" of accidental being; 2) the function, role, and reality of the accidents in sense perception; 3) the fact of human experience of the corruption or deformation of the species of the sacrament. An existence of the accidents without a subject seems not to be possible.

Albert's attempt at a resolution begins with a definition of an accident. *"Esse accidentis est inesse"* ("the being of an accident is its being in") is the "definition" of an accident which Albert accurately attributed to Aristotle.[27] The accident can be defined only from the substance, and so has no proper being. An accident without a subject would be a contradiction in itself.[28] For the problem of how an accident equals *inesse* Albert finds a solution in Avicenna (+1037). "Accident is something understood by the intellect but as dependent on the subject."[29] If the accident does depend upon the being of the subject, existing in the manner of adhering, still in its idea it can be thought of as independent of the subject. Albert interpreted the idea of Avicenna that adherence does not belong to the "concept" of the accident and so is not a constitutive element of it. For Avicenna the accident has in terms of its content its own essence, its own proper being.[30] This *"esse essentiae"* is constituted by the principles of its essence.[31] Albert concluded: "So the accident in nature neither acts nor receives from anything without the subject; the subject does not confer, however, the power of acting and receiving but only sustains it....If the accident were without a subject, no doubt it would act and receive on its own."[32]

---

[27] See Aristotle, *Topica,* 102b4-7.

[28] See Albert, *Super Ethica* 1, 1.

[29] *IV Sent.,* d. 12, a. 16 ad 12. "An accident is understood by the intellect basically as something concrete" (*De corpore domini,* d. 6, tr. 1 c. 1).

[30] See B. Wald, "Substanz/Akzidenz, II.B. Hochscholastik, 1. arabische Tradition, a. Avicenna," *Historisches Wörterbuch der Philosophie* 10 (1998): 510.

[31] *IV Sent.,* d.12, a. 16 ad 2 and ad 4.

[32] Ibid., d. 12, a. 10 sol.

Theological Application

Albert next drew out the theological implications from this view of the metaphysics of accident and subject. Through the *virtus divina* present in their being the accidents exist in the sacrament *sine subjecto*. Their ground gives them a natural capability for activity and reception that comes to them *secundum se* and which are not derived from the principles of the substance. This possibility is founded on the distinction mentioned above between the *"esse in subjecto"* and the *"esse essentiae"* (*proprium esse*). The problems of how the accident apart from the subject works on the senses and, for instance how something putrefies are resolved by looking at the proper activity of accidents. The accident itself belongs to itself. Accidents have their own being (*esse essentiae*) and this can be abstracted from their subject, their substance. When there is a real difference between the proper *esse* and inherence, the accidents (on the basis of the *potentia oboedientialis* of the creature towards the activity of the Creator) can be retained in being by *virtus divina*. The being of the accident does not depend on the substance but on the *virtus divina*.[33]

Aristotle does not know this distinction and sees accidents existing only in the subject, i. e., grounded and maintained in the subject. With his rational method of knowing resting upon the natural principles of things he could hardly see accidents in any other way. [34] Albert drew together peripatetic and neo-Platonic lines of tradition mediated in a special way by Avicenna. Consequently this theory is a contribution to the reception of Aristotelian philosophy, even though the Aristotelianism is colored by a neo-Platonism which Albert made fruitful for the explanation of theological contents.

Further Philosophical Precision: the Role of Quantity.

Our reflections need to be slightly expanded. Albert was not content to leave the modes of existing accidents without a subject to the divine omnipotence which would sustain the accidents in their being in place of the *substantia propria*. He would like to find a deeper foundation for sustaining their existence without a subject. He selects the accident of

---

[33] Ibid., d. 12 a. 16, ad 4.

[34] Ibid., d. 12 a. 16, ad secundam viam ad 1.

quantity. This accident holds the immediate inherency of the other accidents, qualities.[35] Only quantity must be sustained in being through the *virtus divina*. The other accidents have their immediate subject in quantity and retain their natural modes of acting. Quantity by its nature exercises a function of sustaining so that it replaces the function of the "ultimate" subject: *loco subjecti* (*substantiae*). As a *virtus divina* holds them in being (*sine subjecto*), there is a certain participation in the mode of being of substance (*per se existere*[36]) without being a substance. To think that quantity can become substance Albert rejected as absurd and laughable.[37]

With this view of the role of quantity Albert aligned himself with other teachers of his time seeking to explain the existence of accidents without a subject and to explain how those accidents through a divine activity in transubstantiation are raised to a higher mode of being (*status altior*).[38] Can this view of the function of quantity find support in Aristotle? Certainly not in any precise sense. Aristotle is the first in antiquity to define quantity, to place quantity in the categories immediately after substance as the opening of the accidents.[39] Albert drawing on Moses Maimonides said that quantity follows immediately after substance.[40] Aristotle gives quantity special place, and that ontological place is also found in the pseudo-Augustinian work (so influential for the Middle Ages) *Categoriae decem ex Aristotele decerptae* from the end of the fourth century. There are reasons why quantity is the first of the accidents as we see the importance of viewing something according to its size.[41] For Averroes (+1198) quantity is the basic disposition of matter which has a certain

---

[35] Ibid., d. 12, a. 16, ad primam viam ad 1.

[36] Ibid., d. 12, a. 16, ad primam viam ad 11.

[37] Ibid., ad primam viam ad 6.

[38] Ibid., d. 12, a. 16.

[39] F. P. Hager, "Quantität, I. Antike," *Historisches Wörterbuch der Philosophie* 7 (Basel: Schwabe, 1989) 1792.

[40] W. Urban, "Quantität, II. Mittelalter," *Historisches Wörterbuch der Philosophie* 7 1792.

[41] *Categoriae decem...* I, 1-5.

independence from substance.[42] Moreover, for Thomas Aquinas quantity is the subject of the immediate inherence of the accidents after transubstantiation, and one could see the influence of Albert here. In short, Albert had a view which lies in the tradition of Aristotle applied to theology

A New Solution: The Later Work, De corpore Domini

It is rather surprising that Albert in a later work *De corpore domin* [43] rejected this solution of the problem of the accidents and did so with an explicit reference to his commentary on Aristotle's *De anima* (1254 to 1257) and *De sensu et sensato* (after 1257).[44] That text (there is no need to reject the authenticity) includes citations of Albert's views and holds some changes of opinion in terms of Aristotle. Albert set aside the view of an elevation of the accidents, particularly quantity, into a higher state of being (a view he strongly presented in the commentary on the *Sentences*). "That an accident is involved with some other reality existing by itself and not through the substance is unintelligible."[45] The reasons supporting this rejected view "are highly improbable and are given without a convincing reason."[46]

Did he have another more reasonable solution?[47] He began with a question central to a theology of the sacraments: what is the purpose of the remaining accidents? Signification. What do they signify? Christ as spiritual food. How do the accidents, the characteristics perceived by the senses, signify this? They give to the senses an image (*species*; *species sen*sibilis) which is then given to the reason as a sign spiritual food. If the accidents remain as signs (*ut signa*) in the sacrament, then

---

[42] Ibid.

[43] In 1279, as Albert was still alive, this work was attributed to him; see A. Kolping, "Die handschriftliche Verbreitung der Messerklärung Alberts des Grossen," *Zeitschrift für Katholische Theologie* 82 (1960): 1-39.

[44] See H. Jorissen, "Messerklärung und Kommuniontraktat – Werke Alberts des Grossen," *Zeitschrift für katholische Theologie* 82 (1960): 41-97.

[45] *De corpore domini*, d. 6, tr 2 c. 1.

[46] Ibid.

[47] Ibid.

they are reduced to their function of sign, and it is enough that they remain in the sacraments to act upon the senses (*secundum quod sunt species in sensum agentes*). He mentioned the view in the second book of his commentary on the *De anima* where he observed that the objects of the senses act not through their materiality, their natural powers, on the senses' organs (for then the image of fire would burn the eye) but they "*per solam formae intentionem*" work intentionally on the senses. They act in that way that a seal leaves in wax an image without leaving metal from the seal.

The idea of "intention" should be briefly explained. It is taken from the Arab commentaries on Aristotle, particularly from Avicenna's.[48] Albert, drawing on the *De anima*, elaborates on this idea by contrasting it to the substantial form. "The form is that which by properly informing gives existence to the formation of matter and a composition of matter and form. Intention, however, is that through which the thing is signified in an individual or universal way according to diverse grades of abstraction. This does not give being to anything, not to the senses when it is in a sense nor to the intellect when it is in it. It makes a notion of the reality. Intention is not a part of the thing like a form but rather is the image of the whole notion of the thing. Intention because it is extracted from the totality is the signification of the whole of which it is predicated."[49] Intention means the immaterial image:[50] the material and sensible object in the senses as it is in the intellect. Through this the object can be perceived and known because of the intellect's high level of abstraction from the senses that draw on the object. Not only the reception but the object received with its relations to the senses and object constitutes perception and knowing.[51]

---

[48] P. Engelhardt, "Intentio," *Historisches Wörterbuch der Philosophie* 4 466-74.

[49] Albert, *De anima*, l. 2, tr 3. c. 4.

[50] "*Forma sensibilis*," "*species sensibilis*," "*similitudo*," "*imago*"; see Anzulewicz, *De forma resultante*, 87, 123, 126.

[51] The *intentio* is *medium quo* or *per quod* of perception and knowing (Albert, *De homine*, tr. 1, q. 34, a. 2; see U. Dähnert, *Die Erkenntnislehre des Albertus Magnus gemessen an den Stufen der 'abstractio'* [Leipzig: Hirzel, 1934] 28-40).

Albert also considered the theory of perception.[52] The working of the perceived objects on the organs of the senses and the images abstracted from the objects touched by the senses are born by the medium before it is received in the organ. There is then by nature a "being of accidents" (immaterial but still a being) which is set apart from its proper subject of inherence. The images of perception and knowing adhere neither in the sense organ nor in some medium.[53] The conclusion is that accidents have in their function as signs a being which is their intentional being.[54] Accidents keep their reality but in an intentional being of perception. "So the senses receive sensed realities according to a spiritual being, separate from what is in matter and a subject according to a spiritual being."[55] In this way accidental forms without a subject can be perceived in the sacrament as they affect the senses.

We see in *De corpore domini* Albert's effort to present in a reasonable way the possibility of accidents without a subject: or better, the possibility of the sacramental accidents in a mode of being without a subject. Aristotle's theory of perception helps him, although that theory is read through the eyes of Avicenna and Averroes and their interpreters.

Conclusion

These observations show that Albert stood in a philosophical-theological tradition that is certainly not one of a "pure" Aristotelianism. How could there be such purity without it being frozen? Nor is his thought an unreflected ecclecticism. Rather he worked to do justice to the intellectual directions of his time as they unfolded through the "new" Aristotle becoming known and through the presence and claims of faith. Taking into account and accepting the

---

[52] See Dähnert; N. H. Steneck, "Albert on the Psychology of Sense Perception," in J. A. Weisheipl, ed., *Albertus Magnus and the Sciences* (Toronto: Pontifical Institute of Mediaeval Studies, 1980) 263-290; Anzulewicz, "Konzeptionen und Perspektiven."

[53] *De corpore domini,* tr 2 c. l.

[54] Ibid. d. 3 tr 4 l.

[55] *IV Sent.,* d. 12, a 16.

contours of ideas, looking at the "*mysteria/excelsa Dei, inquantum possumus*" (as Albert said), his reflection has decisively influenced this line of tradition.

Recent research on Albert shows that he is far from being simply a compiler. He is an independent thinker who lets himself be inspired by previous thinkers in philosophy and theology. Yet, their influence does not keep him apart from progress but stimulates him to reflect on them anew amid the intellectual challenges of his age.

Henryk Anzulewicz

The Priesthood and Religious Life According to Albertus Magnus

Introduction

The question about the significance of St. Albert the Great in intellectual history was looked at intensively before and after his canonization by Pius XI on December 16, 1931.[1] Today new explorations through contemporary historical research are being pursued with increasing precision and clarity.[2] Albert already in his lifetime had a significant reputation in his Order and in circles of public ecclesiastical life. He was invited to the papal curia in Anagni, Rome, Viterbo, and Orvieto and worked in those cities.[3] Popes Alexander IV and Urban IV entrusted him with important assignments (not the least of which was the episcopacy) in Germany and in other areas that spoke German. Secular rulers like the King of France, St. Louis IX, and the German kings like Wilhelm of Holland and Rudolf von Habsburg (to name only the most important) had contact with him and requested his services. Princes and patricians at war with each other – for instance, the archbishops of Cologne Konrad von Hochstaden and Engelbert von Falkenburg and the Cologne citizenry -- requested his mediation, as did other parties involved in conflicts.[4] The political and

---

[1] The bull of canonization *In thesauris sapientiae* of Pope Pius XI is printed in "Litterae Decretales: Sancti Alberti Magni O.P. confessoris pontificis cultus universae praecipitur ecclesiae, addito doctoris titulo," *St. Albertus-Festschrift, Divus Thomas* 10 (1932): 60-18.

[2] Martin Grabmann described the prior history up to 1932 and the situation of the time just before the canonization of Albert in *Der hl. Albert der Grosse. Ein wissenschaftliches Charakterbild* (Munich: Max Hueber, 1932).

[3] Albert's presence in Anagni, Rome, and Viterbo occurs from September, 1256 to Autumn, 1257; the time in Orvieto reaches from early 1261 to early 1263; see Heribert Christian Scheeben, *Albert der Grosse. Zur Chronologie seines Lebens* (Vechta/Leipzig: Otto Harrasowitz, 1931) 40, 46, 65-69.

[4] See Hugo Stehkämper, "*Pro bono pacis*. Albertus Magnus als Friedensmittler und Schiedsrichter," *Archiv für Diplomatik* 23 (1977): 297-382; "Albertus Magnus und politisch ausweglose Situationen in Köln," in Walter Senner, et

parallel ecclesiastical important of St. Albert is not insignificant. As time passes, his achievements in science have found more importance; they are rightly evaluated as epochal and have secured him over time a place in the history of science in the Latin West.[5] His writings and teaching were studied in the Jewish world and also in Byzantium in the fourteenth and fifteenth centuries: parts of his works were translated into Hebrew and Greek. People in the centuries after Albert honored him with the words, "the Great." They celebrated him as the *Doctor universalis,* while the entire Catholic Church honors him as a saint and doctor of the church. Pius XII named him a doctor of the church on December 16, 1941, ten years after his canonization. To counter the mistrust of scientific progress which had led to the incendiary world war with its vast destruction of humanity he was named patron of scholars in the natural sciences. In the words of Pope Pius XII, the person and prayer of St. Albert might "move the hearts and minds of natural scientists to the peaceful and just use of natural things as they research the laws established by God."[6]

Sketching of the greatness of St. Albert in cultural history asks whether one should one not go deeper and ask about the existential reason for his greatness? Is it enough to look at his life's work and evaluate it? Did the forms of being a religious and a priest, forms of life dedicated to God, also give a format to life that makes possible an openness to what was new?

With his entrance into the Dominican Order Albert chose the path and goal of his life and work. The realization of the program that he worked for and achieved in his life -- there we see the true greatness of

---

al., eds., *Albertus Magnus. Zum Gedenken nach 800 Jahren: Neue Zugänge, Aspekt und Perspektiven* (Berlin, 2001) 359-373.

[5] See Hugo Stehkämper, "Uber die geschichtliche Grösse Alberts des Grossen," *Historisches Jahrbuch* 102 (1982): 72-93; Ludger Honnefelder, "Die philosophische geschichtliche Bedeutung Alberts des Grossen," in Ludger Honnefelder, et al, eds., *Albertus Magnus und die Anfänge der Aristotelis-Rezeption im lateinischen Mittelalter* (Münster: Aschendorff, 2005) 249-279.

[6] See Pius XII, "Litterae apostolicae: Sanctus Albertus Magnus, episcopus confessor atque ecclesiae doctor, cultorum scientiarum naturalium coelestis patronus declaratur," *Divus Thomas* 20 (1942): 109-111.

Albert and his holiness -- is the fruit of a radical decision taken as a young man during his time of study in Italy after he met Jordan of Saxony, the Master of the Order of Preaching Brothers.

Albert's decision for a life of faith in service to truth was pursued by living in a religious order with its evangelical poverty and by living as a priest. His decision for a life's journey (which never had one fixed goal) led him to God as the origin and destiny of human existence and of all of creation. This will illumine how the character, the choice of goals, and the spirituality of the Order of Preachers to a considerable extent penetrated Albert.[7] The following pages will concern themselves with what he reflected on and systematically developed in terms of the sacramental life-forms of dedication to God as a priest (only in so far as he received the sacrament of ordination) and as a religious following Christ.

Albert reflected on the sacrament of orders (in Latin *ordo*) and the state of religious life under various aspects in a number of his theological works. Writings that are theological and systematic treat sacrament, jurisdiction, and office. There is a presentation of the sacrament of ordination in the text *On the Sacraments*,[8] in the commentary on the fourth book of the Sentences of Peter Lombard,[9] and in the commentary on the text of Pseudo-Dionysius Areopagita, *On the Ecclesiastical Hierarchy*[10] Important statements on jurisdiction and the role of the priest as the administrator of the sacraments, as *minister Christi*, can be found in the general theology of Albert on the

---

[7] See Wolfram Hoyer, "Die 'ältesten Konstitutionen' des Predigerordens. Einführung und Übersetzung," in Hoyer, ed., *Jordan von Sachsen. Von den Anfängen des Predigerordens* (Leipzig: Benno, 2003), 203-297; Ulrich Engel, ed., *Dominikanische Spirtualität* (Leipzig: Benno, 2000).

[8] *De sacramentis* tr. 8 [Wilhelm Kübel, ed., Alberti Magni, *Opera Omnia* 26 (Münster: Aschendorff, 1958) 135-153.

[9] *IV Sent.*, di. 24 [Borgnet, Alberti Magni, *Opera Omnia* 30 (Paris: 1894) 30-96b].

[10] *Super Dionysium De ecclesiastica hierarchica* cc. 5-6 [Maria Burger, ed., Alberti Magni, *Opera Omnia* 26/2 (Münster: Aschendorff, 1999)]

sacraments and also in the special section on the eucharist[11] as well as in the certainly authentic double work, *On the Mass* and *On the Eucharist.*[12]

In the areas of moral theology and biblical exegesis he treated virtues which he then links to the sacrament of orders and which should be present in a special way in the one receiving ordination.[13] Moral failures, those living a secular life, the misuse of the priestly office by the church's ministers who are called prelates -- these are repeatedly a motive and an object of criticism. He showed his irritation at the ignorance of the clergy, their bad life style, and their avarice.[14] Ambitious Dominicans as well as those who are opposed to philosophy and science were criticized.[15] On the other hand, he said that a theologian (a priest) who has little to offer positively in his personal authority and style of life can, nonetheless, mediate in a trustworthy way teaching about God for the trustworthiness of the mediation rests neither on his authority nor on the strength of his arguments but on divine bestowal.[16] The same goes for the priestly service at the altar

---

[11] *De sacramentis* tr. 1, ed. cit 5 1-16; *IV Sent.,* di 1, art 1-16 [Borgnet, Alberti Magni, *Opera Omnia* 29 (Paris: 1894) 4a-30b].

[12] *Liber de sacrificio Missae. Liber de sacramento Eucharistiae* . On the issue of authenticity see Henryk Anzulewicz, *De forma resultante in speculo des Albertus Magnus* (Münster: Aschendorf, 1999); Hans Jorissen, *Der Beitrag Alberts des Grossen zur theologischen Rezeption des Aristoteles am Beispiel der Transsubstantionslehre, Lectio Albertina* #5 (Münster: Aschendorff, 2002).

[13] See *De natura boni* [Ephrem Filthau, ed., Alberti Magni, *Opera Omnia* 25/1 (Münster: Aschendorff, 1974) 43, 55ff.; *De bono* , tr. 3. q. 3 [Carl Feckes, ed., Alberti Magni, *Opera Omnia* 28 (Münster: Aschendorff, 1951); see the index of words like *praelatus, presbyter, religiosus , sacerdos* in Bernhard Schmidt, ed., *Super Matthaeum*, Alberti Magni *Opera Omnia* , 21/1-2 (Münster: Aschendorff, 1987).

[14] See *De natura boni* 17.

[15] *Super Dionysii epistulas VII* [Paul Simon,ed., Alberti Magni, *Opera Omnia* , 37/2 (Münster: Aschendorff, 1978) 28-32].

[16] *Super Ethica* , lib. 10, lect. 16 [Wilhelm Kübel, ed., Alberti Magni, *Opera Omnia* 14/2 (Münster: Aschendorff, 1987) 36-41].

and for the administration of sacraments. "Without any doubt we must affirm that bad priests offer validly the sacrifice of the Mass and administers the other sacraments. The opposite meaning is an error and must be opposed as if it were a heresy. Christ has given them their power not as something linked to leading a life without fault....Since, however, he did not place them only as administrators of the sacraments but also wanted to show how a minister suitably administers the sacraments in a meritorious way he selected men virtuous in life and gave them knowledge and power. But it is not necessary that the administrators be such, although it is true that if they are not such, they unworthily administer the sacraments to their own perdition."[17] Albert expressed his views even more clearly on this issue when he emphasized that in the Mass the change of the bread and wine into the body and blood of Christ does not take place through the priest but through Christ himself and the corresponding actions and words at the alter.[18] It is the same with the administration of the sacraments: in the sacraments and through them Christ is at work as healer and not just as dispenser.

Albert's ideas on priesthood and religious life, found in his writings on moral theology and the Bible, are interesting and seminal, but we will not remain with them. We want to draw out some central themes of his systematic interpretation of the sacrament of orders; that sacrament is constitutive for the mode of life of priests and religious in the church. In Albert's view, a life formed by ordination can bear rich fruit. We will now focus on Albert's teaching on the priesthood and religious life as drawn from the general section of his theology of the sacraments. Afterwards we will turn to the special section of the treatise on the sacraments to look at his idea of the sacrament of orders in its basic characteristics. We conclude with Albert's interpretation of the individual steps in the sacrament of orders and their source in the early church. A final excursus looks at the commandment of spiritual maturity. We will follow Albert's texts in their chronological order in order to discern any development in his teaching and to do justice to any shift in emphasis.

---

[17] *IV Sent.,* di. 13, art. 29, ed. cit. 387bf.

[18] Ibid. 388a.

A General Theology of Priesthood and Religious Life

Albert develops systematically in his teaching on sacraments general topics touching upon the sacramental priesthood and the priesthood of priests in religious orders.[19] That theology is found in the early work *On sacraments* and in the final redaction of the commentary on the fourth book of the *Sentences* of Peter Lombard.[20] The general section of the early work focuses on the existence, idea, foundation, number, arrangement, grace, variety, and the sacraments of the New Testament in comparison to their forerunners in the Old Testament.[21] In the commentary on the *Sentences* those questions are treated in a different order and more extensively than in the *On the Sacraments*.[22] The individual sacraments are treated in the second part of the treatise on sacraments from the anointing of the sick *(extrema unctio)* to orders. The same differences in detail between the early work and the later commentary appear. Before we look at that presentation, let us return to the general part to single out what are key statements about the priesthood.

For Albert the priesthood is the sacrament of the new covenant. The sacraments according to the view of the scholastic period (particularly that of Hugh of St. Victor) are means of salvation against the consequences of original sin. Christ is a physician for Albert.[23] A

---

[19] *De sacramentis* tr. 8, q. 5, art. 1, ed. cit. 146.

[20] See note 11.

[21] *De sacramentis,* tr 1, 4-7, ed. cit. 1, 4-7.

[22] Albert begins with four introductory questions: the nature of sacraments, the number, the order, and the difference between the grace of the virtues and gifts and the grace of the sacraments. Twelve questions follow beginning with the definition of a sacrament and ending with the difference between the sacraments of the Old and New Testaments.

[23] *De sacramentis* tr. 1, q. 3, ed. cit. 5, 56-63; see Heinrich Weisweiler, *Die Wirksamekeit der Sakramente nach Hugo von St. Viktor* (Freiburg i. Br.: Herder, 1932) 11-22. While Hugh called the sacraments above all "vessels of grace," Albert saw in each sacrament an inner hylomorphic structure (matter and form) and unites it with a form of sacramental causality; the matter is the sign of the sacrament. With the help of Aristotelian philosophy he

priestly ministry of healing belongs to the essence of the priesthood which in the language of the Bible assists "those who do good and punishes evil doers" (*1 Peter* 2:14). Like baptism and eucharist which the Old Testament knows only in anticipating symbols, the sacrament of the priesthood now "in the age of grace"[24] overcomes moral failings. It exists to counter original sin with its consequent wounding of nature. The people of the Old Testament who were conscious of their state of sinfulness needed to recognize and strive for healing and salvation.[25] Alone they could not achieve this because it comes not from the power of nature but from a power lying deeper than nature and its inner laws.[26] The principle of salvation which is the principle of the new creation – for Albert this is clearly Christ.

How to locate the sacrament of the priesthood within the seven sacraments (whose number is fixed from the middle of the twelfth century)?[27] Albert observed first that all the sacraments as sacraments of the church are to be administered only by the church's ministers (*ministri*). There must then be a sacrament that introduces those who have the office of giving the sacraments. That kind of sacrament, "the sacrament of the ministers" (*sacramentum ministrorum),* is according to Albert the sacrament of orders. The power of the keys (*vis clavium*) has its origins in the sacrament of orders but is not here considered.

---

reinterpreted the viewpoint of the ancients and considered them in light of recent viewpoints without rejecting them; see Hans Jorissen, "Materie und Form der Sakramente im Verständnis Alberts des Grossen," *Zeitschrift für Katholische Theologie* 80 [1958]: 267-315).

[24] De sacramentis tr 1, q. 3, ed. cit. 5, 70-72.

[25] De sacramentis tr 1, q. 3, ed. cit. 6, 76-80.

[26] Albert developed this idea in a philosophical way in *On the Nature and the Origin of the Soul* where the creative principle equals the divine intellect (*De natura et origine animae* tr 1 c. 5 [Bernhard Geyer Alberti Magni, *Opera Omnia* 12 (Münster: Aschendorff, 1955), 14, 31-40].
[27] See Bernhard Geyer, "Die Siebenzahl der Sakramente in ihrer historischen Entwicklung," *Theologie und Glaube* 10 (1918): 341-43; H. Anzulewicz, *Die theologische Relevanz des Bildbegriffs und des Spiegelbildmodells in den Frühwerken des Albertus Magnus, Beiträge zur Geschichte der Philosophie des Mittelalters* NF 53 (Münster: Aschendorff, 1999) 31.

Albert was interested mainly in how this sacrament belongs to the sacraments of the church and what is its distinctive position among them.[28] The reason for including orders in the seven sacraments also comes from the necessity for a sacramental (significative and effective) means against sin. The sacrament of orders wards off "spiritual death" and serves the spiritual growth of all believers in the church of Christians.[29] This ecclesial and office-endowing sacrament determines leaders (*praepositi*) "so that we can lead a peaceful and quiet life" (*1 Tim.* 2:2).[30] The priesthood as the sacramental ministry of the church has a social and a personal dimension in its external activity against evil. In terms of evil influencing people Albert calls the sacrament of orders "a repressing means" (*remedium repressivum*) because it contains the power to punish those who do evil and to reward the good.[31]

The efficacy of the sacrament of the priesthood for salvation leads to the theme of the sign of this sacrament. This sacrament leads the person to a future good which is God. He interprets the priesthood in the image of head and members in the body with the head above the members. [32] Linked to head and members is the image of the church as the mystical body of Christ, an explanation of the position and function of the priest. This perspective shows that the sacrament of orders makes its receiver similar to Christ as a priest, that is, as a man of self-sacrifice.[33]

Ranking the sacraments, Albert puts the sacrament of order (as Peter Lombard does) in the sixth place before the sacrament of

---

[28] *De sacramentis* tr. 1, q. 4, ed. cit. 7 74-90. See Franz-Josef Nocke, *Sakrament und personaler Vollzug bei Albertus Magnus* (Munster: Aschendorff, 1967) 223-225.

[29] *De sacramentis* tr. 1, q. 4, ed. cit. 9.

[30] See note 24.

[31] *De sacramentis* tr. 1, q. 4, ed. cit. 9.

[32] Ibid.

[33] *De sacramentis* tr. 1, q. 6, ed. cit. 15.

marriage. The order of the sacraments corresponds to the natural order of causes of spiritual need and illnesses. Sacraments offer means of salvation as real help in a therapeutic sense.[34] The previous, more personal sacraments give Albert a path to the priesthood and empower people to receive ordination. The priesthood is not a general sacrament offered to each believer who can decide to receive it or not, but like the sacrament of marriage it is for particular persons. It has a higher dignity than marriage because it fashions the spiritual conditions for faith and ecclesial life while marriage enables the corporeal and material existence of the church.[35]

Ordination is an ecclesial sacrament whose activity of salvation is not for the recipient but "for others."[36] Still, it has a personal dimension permitting the recipient to take part in the grace of holiness (*gratia gratum faciens*). There is on grace in all the sacraments -- it is what Albert calls the reality of the sacrament (*res sacramenti*). Grace also has variations: they may counter a particular kind of sin or cause of sin. The reception of sacramental grace – it differs from the grace of the virtues and the gifts of the Holy Spirit -- depends upon the inner disposition of the recipient. Only an honest, spiritual person who places no obstacle to the activity of the Holy Spirit receives this grace.[37] Through the grace of the sacrament the recipient is like the Redeemer who has freed men and women from the power of sin and from sufferings consequent upon sin.[38] The grace of the sacramental priesthood makes its recipient like Christ to the extent that Christ is a priest.[39]

---

[34] Ibid. tr. 1, q. 5, ed. cit. 13.

[35] Ibid.

[36] See Nocke, *Sakrament und personaler Vollzug* 220.

[37] *De sacramentis* tr. 1, q. 6, ed. cit. 14.

[38] Ibid., ed. cit.

[39] See note 33.

What sets the sacramental priesthood apart from the priesthood of the Old Testament? Albert treats this in a general way. Drawing on Hugh of St. Victor, he states three differences between the two testaments in terms of this sacrament. First, the sacraments of the new covenant are effective means of salvation for they justify their receivers; second, they are signs of the grace they work; third, they open after the ascension of Christ the gates of heaven for those who receive them. In the Old Testament there are only signs of salvation, and they do not have an efficacy proper to the sacraments of the New Testament.[40] Similarly a treatment with three points drawing explicitly on the view of Hugh of St. Victor in the commentary on the *Sentences* says that the sacraments of the New Testament are signs of grace while those of the Old Testament are not signs of grace but only signs of the sacraments of the new covenant. The sacraments of the church of Christ are signs and causes of salvation; signs of the older covenant are only signs promising a salvation that they do not contain, while those of the new covenant contain and give that salvation.[41] Albert draws on Augustine for a further distinction as he notes the different subjective presuppositions bearing on sacramental praxis: the emotion of fear is dominant in the old covenant and that of love in the new.[42]

Order as the Sacrament of the Mystical Body of Christ

As we have already indicated, Albert separated orders (and marriage) from the five personal sacraments. He described it as an ecclesial sacrament, as the sacrament of the mystical body in general; it serves first the church as a totality and not the individual person.[43] He noted that Peter Lombard treated the *sacramentum ordinis* under two aspects: the administrator and the recipient. In this framework Albert found space for the presentation of his own theological approaches and for a certain creativity and independence in detail.

---

[40] *De sacramentis* tr. 1, q. 7. ed. cit. 15.

[41] *IV Sent.* di. 1, art. 15, ed. cit. 29b.

[42] Ibid.

[43] *IV Sent.* di. 24, Prologue, ed. cit. 30a.

From that network of themes only the first and most important is here presented, deserving special attention not only because of its appearance in the history of theology but also because of its systematic relevance for the contemporary understanding of the sacramental priesthood.

Conceptual Clarifications: Priesthood as Sacrament, Jurisdiction, and Office

In terms of Albert's exposition of the sacrament of orders what is contained in the early work *On Sacraments* is primarily and formally different from the presentation of the commentary on the *Sentences*. For the second work Albert chose a different arrangement of the material and a more attentive exposition with depth and breadth of reflection. While he developed his teaching in the early work directly and with a certain logical order that balances its themes, later he saw himself more bound to writing a commentary. It is striking that in the early work the power of the keys is joined to the priesthood while in the commentary on the *Sentences* the keys find their place in the interpretation of penance and is discussed there (as happens in Lombard's *Sentences*). What is the relationship of Albert's idea of priesthood from the early work to the commentary on the *Sentences*?

Which terms does Albert use for the sacrament of priestly orders? How does he define that sacrament? To compare *De sacramentis* with the commentary on Lombard and Pseudo-Dionysius' *Hierarchica* is to see that Albert consistently used the Latin term *ordo* first for the sacrament of orders which includes spiritual jurisdiction (*spiritualis potestas)* and office (*officium*). Albert borrowed this terminology of the priesthood from two definitions of Peter Lombard. In the first definition the sacrament of the priesthood is "a certain seal, a certain temple through which spiritual power and the office of the ordained is given."[44] The second approach is a spiritual character which empowers spiritual power.[45] The term "seal" (*signaculum*) is for Albert part of the sacramental character which the second phrase mentions.[46] Here Albert found himself thinking in the direction of

---

[44] Peter Lombard, *Sententiae,* Bk. 4, di. 24, c. 13.

[45] *De sacramentis* tr. 8, q. 1, ed. cit. 135.

Alexander of Hales,[47] while Thomas Aquinas set aside this view and interpreted the word *signaculum* as that "which bears externally what is a sign and cause of inner power.[48] The terms of "degree" and "step" (*gradus*) appear as synonyms for an order. Albert interpreted a degree of an order in the sense of an admission to a spiritual dignity.[49]

The commentary on the *Sentences* gives a certain expansion to the sacrament of orders which has a positive and harmonic relationship to the earlier work. He introduced a further definition, something from a "previous teacher" – in fact, it comes from Alexander of Hales. "Order is the sacrament of spiritual power ordained to an office which is placed in the church for the sacrament of com-munion."[50] Albert did not interpret the seal and sacramental character as the essence of the sacrament of orders but preferred the power and the office given through it. There is no doubt that with the sacrament of communion he meant the eucharist, although this is not mentioned further and no further connection to orders is given.

Without going into the tripartite structure of the sacrament of orders,[51] it is clear that he saw the essence of this sacrament, the existential ground of ordination, in the sacramental seal as the sign and the cause of the grace of the sacrament. This seal is not only a

---

[46] Ibid.

[47] Alexander of Hales, *Glossa in IV Sent., di. 24, nr. 2e.h* (Quarrachi Florentiae: Ex Typographia Colegii S. Bonaventurae, 1957) 400, 1-7, 21-23.

[48] Thomas Aquinas, *IV Sent.,* di. 24, 1, sol. 2, ad 1 (cf. *Summa theologiae, Supplement,* q. 34, a. 2); see Ludwig Ott, *Das Weihsakrament* (Frei burg: Herder, 1969) 75-76.

[49] *De sacramentis* tr. 8, q. 1, ed. cit. 135; 136.

[50] Ibid.; see Ott, *Das Weihsakrament...*76.

[51] This consists of the sign of the sacrament alone (*signum tantum*), the "reality of the sacrament" (*res tantum*), and the reality and sign together (*res et signum*) which Albert designated as the mediation (*medium*) between the reality and the sign of the sacrament and stated to be what is essential in the sacrament (*essentia sacramenti*) (*De sacramentis* tr. 8 q. 1, ed. cit. 136).

mark giving spiritual distinction but the sign of a certain distinction belonging to the priest and at the same time the ground of spiritual power. Thomas Aquinas seems to agree with his teacher here.[52] This power (like every other power according to the Apostle Paul [53]) has a place in an order within corresponding liturgical and canonical prescriptions. The office of priesthood is linked to power, for that office exists mainly to further the exercise of the power contained in the sacraments.[54] Each recipient of orders has spiritual power according to the degree of the order received, although the exercise of each power, however, is reserved to ecclesiastical administration. The church observes and regulates in various circumstances the spiritual power it has in light of its main concern: the building up of the people of God in love. Every monk ordained has spiritual power but the exercise of that power through the monk is limited (but not negated).[55]

With regards to the office of priest (belonging as it does to the essence of the sacrament of orders) Albert did little more than explain terminology. He began with the secular idea of office from the Stoa and Cicero and states that *officium* is a "suitable activity of a particular person according to the customs and institutions of the country." [56] The theological employment of this secular idea may have been suggested by Alexander of Hales. [57] Albert noted the parallels between state and community and the church and God. [58]

---

[52] See note 48.

[53] *Letter to the Romans* 13:1.

[54] *De sacramentis* tr. 8, q. 1, ed. cit. 136.

[55] *De sacramentis* tr. 8, q. 1, ed. cit. 136.

[56] *De sacramentis* tr. 8, q. 1, ed. cit. 135.

[57] Alexander of Hales, *Glossa in IV Sent.,* di. 24, nr. 2i, ed. cit. 400.

[58] *De sacramentis* tr. 8, q. 1, ed. cit. 136.

The Division and Levels of One Sacrament

Order is one sacrament. It has, however, several degrees. Albert along with most theologians of the High Middle Ages accepted seven orders in contrast to the nine given by significant canonists.[59] Thus the sacrament of orders enjoys some diversity and separation.[60] This does not mean the unity of the sacrament should be set aside but that its variety should be explored and rationally explained. There are two models for such an explanation: a logical division which sees various kinds in one genus, and an ontological one which treats a totality in its components.[61] He prefers the second model where sacrament is seen as a virtual totality preceeding each of its parts. This model whose source Albert found in Boethius[62] is also found in writers on grammar like Priscan who saw the concept of *ordo* as a kind of totality (*quoddam totum*) which can contain numerous partial power or partial potencies.[63] A grammatical interpretation of *ordo* fits with that of Boethius affirming a virtual totality where the totality flows into the parts, and Albert kept the resolution of the question of the unity and diversity of the sacrament of order at the ontological level.

After the issue of there being one sacrament of orders with seven degrees of orders it remains to see which stages of orders exist and what is the ministry of each.

The theologians and the canonists did not agree on the number, and Hugh of St. Cher and Raymond of Peñafort, both Domninicans and educated in theology and canon law, affirm nine, Albert represents the majority of theologian who see seven "individual orders" (*ordines singulares*). They make up an office with different facets. Here we will look briefly at the individual orders.

---

[59] See Ott *Das Weihsakrament* 48, 78f.

[60] *De sacramentis* tr. 8, q. 2, ed. cit. 138.

[61] Ibid.

[62] See Boethius, *De divisione,* [John Magee, ed. (Leiden: Brill, 1998) 8, 9-16].

[63] *De sacramentis* tr. 8, q. 2, ed. cit. 138.

1) The first and lowest order is the porter. With ordination the porter (*ostiarius*, or less frequently, *ianitor*) is given the ministry of supervising the doors of the church. According to Isidore of Seville he has the power to give access to the church and its shrines to those who are suitable and to keep away those not suitable. Those unsuited are for Albert not those in the state of mortal sin but those who are excommunicated or those doing public penance for evil actions. He corrected the understanding of Isidore of Seville as he also gave to the porters the ministry of watching over all the places where the sacraments are celebrated.

2) The second order is that of the reader (*lectoratus*) who receives a spiritual power for the ministry of reader. This power and office are for the readings and explanations of prophecies for the people.[64]

3) The third order is the exorcist (*exorcista*). The recipient receives the power to keep evil spirits (demons) away from human bodies, to drive them out of people, or to reduce their power which is the source of sinfulness and an obstacle for receiving the sacraments.[65]

4) The fourth order is the acolyte (*acolytha*) who takes care of lighting the candles and other instruments of illumination. As a sign of its radiating material light, he assists at the reading of the Gospel so that the darkness and the hiddenness of the past prophecies can be set aside.

5) The fifth order is the subdiaconate (*subdiaconatus*) which serves at the altar particularly in terms of the eucharist. The subdeacon has the power to touch the eucharistic gifts and vessels, to receive them from the people and to take them to the altar.

6) The ministry of the deacon (*diaconatus*) has mainly to do with the liturgy of the Mass. There is the reading of the gospel and then the service of the eucharist directly at the altar. He receives the offertory gifts from the people out of the hands of the subdeacon and arranges them on the altar. He serves the priest at the consecration as he hands

---

[64] *De sacramentis* tr. 8, q. 2, ed. cit. 136; *IV Sent.*, di 24, art. 21, ed. cit. 57a-58b.

[65] For the following see *De sacramentis* tr. 8, q. 2, ed. cit. 137, 138, 139. See Ulrich Horst, *Bischöfe und Odensleute. Cura principalis und via perfectionis in der Ekklesiologie des hl. Thomas von Aquin* (Berlin: Akademie Verlag, 1999) 49.

to him the host and the chalice with wine. He receives the paten by kissing it and gives it to the subdeacon. He prepares the corporal and puts the hosts to be consecrated on it. After the consecration he distributes communion to the people. The ministry of the deacon and all his activities are for Albert aimed at the eucharist.

7) The last and highest level of sacramental ordination is the presbyter (*presbyteratus*), ordination to the priesthood. The most important power received at ordination by the priest is the power to consecrate the eucharist. Added to that is the power of the keys. The name of this office comes from the Greek, *presbyteratus*, although later Albert used the word coming from the Latin-Christian tradition, *sacerdotium* and *sacerdos.* The power of the keys of the priest and the powers of all the orders below the priesthood are aimed at the eucharist, indeed, at the consecration. The consecration is the primary and important activity of the priesthood. The power of the keys and other powers of the individual levels are at work to insure the worthy reception of the eucharist.

The discussion of different orders leads to the question of the sacramental character. His view was that this spiritual mark was present in the lower orders. Because there are seven orders, the question emerges whether the person receives seven characters. Albert's solution seems theologically and philosophically plausible and suitable. The sacramental seal touches the person at each ordination.[66] Since all are aimed at the priesthood, with the priesthood's seal there is a sacramental completion of the sacrament of orders. The other seals likes their stages are dispositions for the sacramental priest-hood.[67]

The Source of the Sacrament of Orders and Origins in the Early Church.

Along with Peter Lombard and others in the teaching tradition of the church Albert led the sacrament of orders and its seven stages back to Christ as their founder. Through various activities Christ forecast and

---

[66] *De sacramentis* tr. 8, q. 2, ed. cit. 136; see Ott, *Das Weihsakrament* 75.

[67] *IV Sent.,* di. 24, art. 34, ed. cit 75a; see Nocke, *Sakrament und personaler Vollzug* 226-227.

founded it.[68] "The porter is like Christ who drove the unworthy out of the temple with a whip he made. The reader is like Jesus who read the book of the Prophet Isaiah and said that this prophecy was fulfilled in him: 'The Spirit of the Lord is upon me because he has anointed me.'"[69] The exorcist is like Jesus who drove demons out of people and who with spittle loosened the tongue and ears of one blocked: 'Ephata. Be opened.'[70] The acolyte ministers to the light of the world. 'I am the light of the world. Who follows me does not walk in darkness.'[71] The subdeacon recalls him who put a towel around his waste and washed the feet and hands of the first priests, his disciples.[72] The deacon is the one to takes the consecrated bread from the table and gives it to the disciples.[73] The priest changes the bread and wine into his body and blood."

All the orders existed in the early church. Albert emphasized this. The lesser orders were linked to the diaconate because in the first communities there was a small number of *ministri* available and the need for all of them was not so great since most Christian led a holy life. In the course of time the number of those in the *ministry* grew while the piety of the Christians declined. Albert saw this as the reason for the decision to divide the orders, and he knows that in many churches the first four are given in the same ceremony.[74]

The Command of Perfection.

A further issue is holiness. Why are these orders called "holy"? Not because they come from the authority of the early church in its

---

[68] *De sacramentis* tr. 8, q. 7, ed. cit. 151.

[69] *Isaiah* 61: 1; *Luke* 4: 18.

[70] *Mark* 7: 32-35.

[71] *John* 8:12.

[72] *John* 13: 4-5.
[73] *Matthew* 26:26-28.

[74] *IV Sent.,* di. 24, art. 36, ed. cit.

holiness or in its importance but because they come from the holiness which, if few have it, all recipients have professed in their vows, confessing themselves disciples of sanctity.[75]

The three higher orders – subdiaconate, diaconate, and presbyterate – have the attribute of "holy" because they require of their recipient a holy life, for they serve the gift of that sacrament which holds and bestows holiness. Albert linked a holy life first with a perfect and perduring continency and chastity;[76] in the Latin church of the West (differently than in the Eastern churches) the priesthood requires celibacy and is solemnly professed.[77] Those two virtues are basic for they are the presupposition for the devotion and for the ascent of the human person to God. Albert (following Boethius) saw sensual pleasure as an earthly chain which binds the person to what is low in nature and hinders striving to higher perfection.[78] Grace is given in the sacrament of orders grace to bestow power for a holy life. Correspondingly the subdeacon because of his order has the virtue of chastity; the deacon has chastity in its purifying form; the priest is chaste in the form of having been purified.[79] Albert without mentioning it draws this interpretation of holiness from Plotinian-Macrobian teaching of virtue[80] which he uses often in his moral

---

[75] Ibid.

[76] Albert sees chastity and continency as sub-virtues of temperance; De bono , tr 3, qq. 2-3, ed. cit. 135-186.

[77] IV Sent., di. 24, art. 28, ed. cit. 66b.

[78] IV Sent., di. 37, art. 3, ed. cit. 384a.

[79] Ibid.

[80] Albert is acquainted with the teaching on virtue of Plotinus through Macrobius (a Roman official of the fifth century and a mediator of Platonic thought) and his Commentary on the Dream of Scipio; see Jörn Müller, Natürliche Moral und philosophische Ethik bei Albertus Magnus (Munster: Aschendorff, 2001) 193.

theology.[81] He joined it to the teaching of Pseudo-Dionysius on the purifying, illuminating, and perfecting functions of deacon, presbyter, and bishop. He brought his own interpretation to the Dionysian view of the three higher orders.[82]

All people are called to some kind of perfection (*perfectio sufficientiae*) which Albert developed in his theology of virtues); priests and religious and those who have received the sacrament of orders are called to a particular perfection which they have professed.[83] Albert paid attention to the perfection of the church leaders (*praelati*), those working in pastoral ministry (*pastores*), as well as to preachers (*praedicatores*). Preachers speak the Word of God "utterly independent of a local pastoral ministry" and do not have that local pastoral office."[84] A binding, high measure of perfection obliges the bearers of ecclesiastical leadership. The Scripture says that there is no greater love than to lay down one's life for his friend.[85] Ecclesiastical prelates are bound to this command of Jesus on the basis of their ministry (*ex officio*). Preachers are bound to it on the basis of their preaching (*ex actu*) and upon the holy life which confirms their preaching.[86]

---

[81] *De bono* tr. 3, prologue, ed. cit. 134, 33ff.; see Müller, *Naturliche Moral...* 145-51, 192-197.

[82] *IV Sent.*, di. 37, art 3, ed. cit. 384b.

[83] *III Sent.*, di. 29, art. 8 [Borgnet, Alberti Magni, *Opera Omnia* 28) 560a-b].

[84] See Jean Longère, "Predigt," *Lexikon des Mittelalters* 7 (1995) 173.

[85] *III. Sent.*, di. 29, art 8, ed. cit. 560b.

[86] Ibid. 561a,

Rudolf Schieffer

Albertus Magnus. Mendicancy and Theology
in Conflict with Episcopacy

The activity of Albert of Lauingen as bishop in Regensburg was only a brief episode in the long life of the *"Doctor universalis."* Nonetheless, in contrast to other, possibly more fruitful, theological and philosophical periods that segment of Albert's biography is rather precisely documented, for the reality of being a bishop at that time was immediately linked to the production of documentary sources, and they are eminently suited to yield, even centuries later, information that can be precisely dated.[1]

Albert Becomes a Bishop.

We know that on January 5, 1260, Pope Alexander IV in Anagni approved the preparation of documents to be sent to Albert as well as to the Cathedral Chapter and to the secular administrators of diocesan institutions of the Regensburg church in which he made know to the Dominican professor at Cologne his elevation to the episcopal chair of St. Wolfgang and held his future flock to obligatory obedience toward their new shepherd.[2] Just a few weeks later, in March of 1260, Albert,

---

[1] Basic works for Albert's biography and for its written sources are: P. de Loë, *De vita et scriptis B. Alberti Magni, Analecta Bollandiana* 19 (1900) 257-284; 20 (1901) 273-316; 21 (1902) 361-371; H. C. Scheeben, *Albert der Grosse. Zur Chronologie seines Lebens* (Vechta, 1931); for the period in Regensburg see J. Staber, "Albertus Magnus als Bischof von Regensburg," *Verhandlungen des Historischen Vereins von Oberpfalz und Regensburg* 106 (1966): 175-193; P. Mai, "Albertus Magnus als Bischof von Regensburg," G. Schwaiger, P. Mai, eds., *Beiträge zur Geschichte des Bistums Regensburg* 14 (Regensburg, 1980) 23-39; G. Schwaiger, "Der heilige Albertus Magnus. Kirchenlehrer, Bischof von Regensburg (1260-1262)," G. Schwaiger, ed., *Lebensbilder aus der Geschichte des Bistums Regensburg* (Regensburg, 1989) 156-167; J. Gruber, "Albertus Magnus -- ein Dominikaner auf dem Regensburger Bischofsstuhl (um 1200-1280)," K. Dietz, G. H. Waldherr, eds., *Berühmte Regensburger. Lebensbilder aus zwei Jahrtausenden* (Regensburg, 1997) 70-78.

[2] For documents in print see P. Mai, "Urkunden Bischof Alberts II. von Regensburg (1260-1262)," in *Verhandlungen des Historischen Vereins für Oberpfalz und Regensburg* 107 (1967): 7-45, particularly 11f. Nr. 1; 12f. Nr 2; here according to the Passau textual tradition, but also textually supported by the papal registers (*Les registres d'Alexandre IV* t. 3, A. Coulon, ed. (Paris,

appearing in a first document as being in Würzburg on the way to his new place of activity, is designated as "elected and confirmed for the church in Regensburg" and is already arranging some of the affairs of the parish church in Eger which belongs to that diocese.[3] On April 9th and May 10th in Regensburg, he, the chosen future bishop, sent documents to the Cistercians in Waldsassen and to the Benedictines in Prüfening[4] and sometime before July 16th he received episcopal consecration. From the day of consecration itself (the precise date is not stated) comes a decree for the Abbey of Niederaltaich,[5] and between the sixteenth and the thirty-first of July there is a series of three documents marked with the full title of bishop in Regensburg: they benefit the cathedral chapter, the hospital of St. Catherine, and the Teutonic Knights in the city.[6] Soon after, Bishop Albert seems to have traveled to the Alpine area, perhaps to inspect the property of the Regensburg diocese in the Tyrol;[7] at any rate in September (we do not have the date) he is in Sterzing south of the Brenner Pass along with Duke Ludwig II of Bavaria and the Duke's brother-in-law Count Meinhard II of Tyrol.[8] On September 25th, he is on his return route, in Landau on the Isar river amid his episcopal brothers holding a synod presided over by Ulrich, Archbishop of Salzburg,[9] while on October 13th he consecrated the chapel of St. Kolomann near the church of St.

1953) 99, Nrs. 3058, 3059). The letter to Regensburg is reprinted in *Monumenta_Germaniae Historica [MGH]. Epistolae saeculi XIII selectae*, C. Rodenberg, ed., 3 (Berolini [Berlin], 1894) 465f., Nr. 504 (more complete than in Mai); see A. Potthast ed., *Regesta Pontificum Romanorum inde ab a. post Christum natum MCXCVIII ad a._MCCCIV* (Berolini [Berlin], 1875) Nr. 17737, 17738

[3] Mai, *Urkunden* 13f. Nr 3; no date given.

[4] Ibid. 14f., Nr. 4; Ibid. 15f. Nr. 5.

[5] Ibid. 16, Nr. 6.

[6] Ibid. 16f., Nr. 7; Ibid. 18, Nr. 8; Ibid. 19f., Nr. 9.

[7] Thus Mai, *Albertus* 34. Differing from this opinion is my view that the journey would have taken place between August 19 (Mai, *Urkunden* 20f. Nr. 10) and September 25 when the Landau synod took place (see note 9 below).

[8] See Mai. *Urkunden* 22f., Nr. 113.

[9] Ibid. 21f., Nr. 11, 12.

Emmeram in Regensburg.[10] The subsequent months offer the most probable period for a journey to Vienna – the city was controlled at that time by the King of Bohemia, Ottokar II – where Albert had an important role in renewing imperial privileges for the German Order in Austria.[11] Three documents from February 22nd, 1261 [12] – one of them confirms the reform statutes for the Benedictines given by Pope Gregory IX published in 1237 [13] – put him back in Regensburg.

Subsequently, however, Albert's traces become less clear. A stone inscription makes it certain that he consecrated a church at Lerchenfeld not far east of Regensburg.[14] He is one of the senders of a common declaration by the suffragan bishops of Salzburg in favor of the Metropolitan Ulrich whom they support in his bitter conflict with his deposed predecessor Philip.[15] That undated text (sent not to the pope but to the cardinals of the Roman church) implies that it comes from a gathering that took place somewhere in Bavaria; the death of Pope Alexander IV on May 25th, 1261 is mentioned but not the election of his successor Urban IV on August 29th.[16] All the evidence implies that Bishop Albert himself brought those documents to the Curia in Viterbo, for a journey there occupied most of 1261.[17] In

---

[10] Ibid. 23, Nr. 14.

[11] Ibid. 24ff., Nr. 16.

[12] Ibid. 27ff., Nr. 17-19.

[13] *Les registres de Grégoire IX*, t. 2. (Paris, 1907) 317ff., Nr. 3045bis; on their wide distribution see F. J. Felten, "Die Ordensreformen Benedikts XII. unter institutionengeschtlichem Aspekt," G. Melville ed., *Institutionen und Geschichte. Theoretische Aspekte und mittelalterliche Befunde* (Cologne, 1992) 369-435; particularly 374.

[14] See Mai, *Albertus,* 36.

[15] For the background of this see H. Dopsch, "Premsyl Ottokar II. und das Erzstift Salzburg," in *Ottokar-Forschungen, Jahrbuch für Landeskunde von Niederösterreich NF* 44/45 (Vienna, 1979) 470-508, particularly 484ff.; H. Wagner, "Von Interregnum bis Pilgrim von Puchheim," *Geschichte Salzburgs* 1/1 H. Dopsch, ed., (Salzburg, 1983) 437-486; particularly 439ff.

[16] Mai, *Urkunden* 40f., Nr. 20 (not accurate in establishing the dating).

[17] *Annales S. Rudberti Salisburgenses ad a. 1261, MGH SS* 9, 796.

Regensburg on December 23, 1261, the Provost and the Dean of the Cathedral Chapter and its Vicar were expressly acting in place of the absent bishop,[18] while Albert in a document of February 25, 1262 is presumed to be still the bishop in office,[19] although he had already been busy at the Curia working to get his resignation approved. When precisely his application to resign from the office of bishop of Regensburg was accepted we do not know, although four letters (similar in their text) of May 11, 1262 from Pope Urban to the cathedral chapter, the clergy, the people in the city and the diocese, as well as to the secular administrators of church institutions and the vassals of the Regensburg church confirm the resignation of Albert and give papal approval to the election of his successor, the previous dean of the cathedral chapter, Leo, an election by the chapter that had already taken place.[20]

This is the sequence of facts offered by dependable sources of the thirteenth century. For us today that narrative of an episcopate of barely two years seems astonishing and calls for some explanation. Why had the great theologian, little more than sixty years old,[21] ascended to the pinnacle of hierarchy? And why did he give up its successful realization? Setting aside his office, however, as far as we know, took place largely without rumor or discussion. On the other hand, it had been with some trouble that Albert was raised to the dignity of being bishop of Regensburg, and that process occupies us now.

---

[18] Mai, *Urkunden* 42, Nr. 22.

[19] Ibid. 43, Nr. 23.

[20] T. Ried, *Codex chronologico-diplomaticus episcopatus Ratisbonensis* 1 (Ratisbonae, 1816) 464ff., Nr. 489 using the original; see Potthast, *Regesta* (note 2) Nr. 18309 which is not found in the papal registers. On his successor see P. Mai, "Bischof Leo Tundorfer. Ein Regensburger Patriziersohn auf der Kathedra des hl. Wolfgang (1262 -1277)," in Georg Schwaiger, ed., *Der Regensburger Dom. Beiträge zu seiner Geschichte* (Regensburg, 1976) 69-95.

[21] On Albert's age see Scheeben, *Albert* 4f.

Papal Power and Canonical Election.

The pope fashioned Albert's elevation. Such an act, however, is not as obvious as it might be to a modern observer. In the thirteenth century the Apostolic See was in its first period of influencing appointments to episcopal sees in Germany.[22] The controversy over investiture had resulted in blocking the previously dominant influence of secular rulers and normally in excluding them. The ancient principle of a canonical election by clergy and people had, , had the practical effect of giving an exclusive privilege to the canons of the cathedral to decide, as unanimously as possible, who was to be their new shepherd.[23] The capitulars of the cathedral, mainly coming from the leading families of the nobility in the region, would measure people by their own social status, and so their choice in the selection of bishops would be decidedly aristocratic.[24] That was reinforced by a sensitivity to the role of the bishop being a prince, albeit a spiritual one, in the empire. The princely aspect of episcopal office became increasingly important after the Concordat of Worms, and required a bishop to have a suitable origin and support in terms of social status. The family of someone like Albertus Magnus was of lower noble lineage and did not reside in Bavaria,[25] and so he would have appeared to the Regensburg canons not normally electable.

Precisely the extraordinary aspect of this situation – a Dominican friar who is also a scholar receives this high position thanks to the papacy – is particularly suited for illustrating by means of this particular case the general conditions of the age that required the ever

---

[22] See P. Landau, "Der Papst und die Besetzung der Bischofsstühle," *Zeitschrift für evangelisches Kirchenrecht* 37 (1992): 241-254; particularly 248f.

[23] See K. Ganzer, "Zur Beschränkung der Bischofswahl auf die Domkapitel in Theorie und Praxis des 12. und 13. Jahrhunderts," *Zeitschrift der Savigny-Stiftung für Rechtsgeschichte, Kanonistische Abteilung* 57 (1971): 22-82; 58 (1972) 166-197; H. Müller, *Der Anteil der Laien an der Bischofswahl. Ein Beitrag zur Geschichte der Kanonistik von Gratian bis Gregor IX* (Amsterdam, 1977).

[24] See M. Borgolte, *Die mittelalterliche Kirche* (Munich, 1992) 43ff., 102ff.

[25] See A. Layer, "Albert von Lauingen und sein Geschlecht," *Jahrbuch des Historischen Vereins Dillingen an der Donau* 81 (1979): 31-40.

expanding influence of the Curia Romana. The cathedral chapter with
its right of election retained the autonomy of its decision only as long
as its members remained relatively in accord with each other. In the
case of disagreement a mechanism for unity fell into place, one
recognized by all sides involved: an appeal to a higher instance. After
the discrediting of royal power, the higher instance could only be the
authority of the papacy. To remain with this particular case, a similar
situation had appeared in 1226/27 when after a contentious episcopal
election a group of canons went to Rome and presented to Gregory IX
their grievances. They urged the pope to set aside the selection just
made in Regensburg and to mandate a new election in which only the
members of the chapter who had come to the pope could participate.
[26] When bishop Siegfried (he had been elected) died, a unanimous
election still appeared impossible, and the papal legate, who was
traveling around Bavaria to counter the political party supporting the
imperial Staufer family, appeared on the scene and was able to make a
final decision for the new bishop, Albert I.[27] That earlier Albert's
various disputes and massive acts of violence[28] reached a point where
the cathedral chapter in 1258 initiated a process at the *Curia Romana*
against him. The result was that the guilty bishop had to resign in the
following year. The cathedral chapter chose the Propst Heinrich von
Lerchenfeld as his successor, but he declined the election. Thus no
other way was seen but to hand over the selection to the pope.[29] The
elevation of Albertus Magnus (Albert II), someone outside of all the
parties involved, by Alexander IV at the beginning of 1260 is clearly

---

[26] See A. Diegel, *Der päpstliche Einfluss auf die Bischofswahlen in Deutschland
während des 13. Jahrhunderts* (Berlin, dissertation, 1932) 59; K. Ganzer,
*Papsttum und Bistumsbesetzungen in der Zeit von Gregor IX. bis Bonifaz VIII.
Ein Beitrag zur Geschichte der päpstlichen Reservationen* (Cologne/Graz,
1968) 125; K. Hausberger, *Geschichte des Bistums Regensburg* 1 (Regensburg,
1989) 121.

[27] See Diegel, *Einfluss* 60; Ganzer, *Papsttum* 138; Hausberger, *Geschichte* 123f.

[28] Hausberger, *Geschichte* 124ff.; D. Hagen, "Die politische Behauptung des
Hochstifts Regensburg zwischen Reich, Bayern und Bürgertum im 13.
Jahrhundert," P. Mai, K. Hausberger, eds., *Beiträge zur Geschichte des Bistums
Regensburg* 31 (Regensburg, 1997) 7-54.

[29] See Hausberger, *Geschichte* 127f.

explained by an unease over a longer vacancy.[30] This is, nonetheless, the first direct selection of a bishop of Regensburg by a pope. How this unusual procedure affected and formed the mentality of those witnessing it can be seen from the events following the resignation of this second Albert in 1262. Pope Urban IV set aside his own determination of a successor (something possible for him to do) and required that the Regensburg chapter proceed to a new election which, as mentioned above, chose the Dean Leo. But now Leo hesitated: he would not assume this office until the Pope had given his confirmation which quickly arrived.[31]

What reasons led the pope at the beginning of the year 1260 to expect that Albert could master the manifestly difficult situation in Regensburg? The reasons can be found with some clarity in the letter of appointment whose basic text went in similar forms to Cologne and to Regensburg.[32] To the future bishop are ascribed the virtues of "*probitas*" and "*prudential*," and also the concrete goal of a "*reformatio*" of that disturbed church is stated.[33] In the Regensburg version the future bishop is announced as one who will bring "*sententia...in rebelles*" ("a judgment against the rebellious").[34] The following central sentence (from the version sent to Regensburg) presents a link between the personality of Albert and his new assignment: "Since the same friar has drunk so deeply of the streams of salvific teaching ("*salutifere fluenta doctrine*") coming from the source of divine law ("*de legis divine fonte*"), and since the fullness of this knowledge is active in his breast ("*eiusdem doctrine in suo pectore vigeat plenitudo*") and in those things which are of God the judgment of reason is at his command ("*sibique presto sit in his que Dei sunt iudicium rationis*"), the unshakable hope is nourished that in the aforementioned church which in both spiritual and temporal orders is

---

[30] For sources see note 2 in this article; on the legal problematic see Diegel, *Einfluss* 77f.; Ganzer, *Papsttum* 246; Hausberger, *Geschichte* 128.

[31] See note 20 of this article and Diegel, *Einfluss* 71; Ganzer, *Papsttum* 260; Hausberger, *Geschichte* 130.

[32] See note 2 above.

[33] Mai, *Urkunden* 12.

[34] *MGH, Epp. saec. XIII* 3, 466.

deformed in many ways ("*in spiritualibus et temporalibus...multipliciter deformata*") he can heal the wounds and remove the damage through the zeal of his circumspection ("*per sue diligentie studium*").[35]

Here without doubt, carefully chosen words beyond the usual routine language of the chancery refer to the reputation of high learning attributed to Albert: not, however, in the sense that the church in Regensburg merits a leading theological thinker and teacher as such but more that he as an established authority will be able, more than others, to overcome the divisions through a "*iudicium rationis*". The pope's confidence in Albert arose from personal contacts occurring three years earlier during Albert's time at the Curia in Anagni and Rome.[36] Certainly he knew too that Albert had the experience of three years in office as the leader of the Dominican province, Teutonia,[37] and he could have heard that Albert had lived for a while in Regensburg.[38] Above all it must be recalled that already in 1260 Albert had emerged as a judge and mediator of peace.[39] Through the agreement of 1258 in Cologne (the "*Grosser Schied*") he had brought about a modus vivendi between the archbishop and the citizenry.[40] The legal consequences of that decision had had ramifications for Alexander's Curia in Anagni and occasioned a confirmation from the Pope on October 18, 1259, and presumed precise information about those recent political events in Cologne.[41]

---

[35] Ibid.

[36] Scheeben, *Albert* 43ff.

[37] See Ibid., 36ff.

[38] See *I*bid., 18ff. for the uncertain chronology.

[39] See H. Stehkämper, "*Pro bono pacis.* Albertus Magnus als Friedensmittler und Schiedsrichter," *Archiv für Diplomatik* 23 (1977): 297-382.

[40] See M. Groten, *Köln im 13. Jahrhundert. Gesellschaftlicher Wandel und Verfassungsentwicklung* (Cologne, 1995): for the "*Kleiner Schied*" from 1252, see 121ff.; for the "*Grosser Schied*" from 1258, see 184ff.

[41] *MGH Epp. saec XIII* 3, 461f., Nr. 500; see Groten, *Köln* 198. Another example of a mediatior is the Dominican cardinal Hugh of St. Cher who was active with Albert in drafting an agreement (the "*Kleiner Schied*") in Cologne in 1252 and who on February 20, 1252, as a legate from Anagni, met with the Archbishop

If this was the cause of Albert's nomination, it fits the picture that one has in general of the basic conditions of episcopal existence in the high and late Middle Ages.[42] To do justice to the daily demands of leading a diocese and its territory, a man needed administrative perdurance, diplomatic ingenuity, political and (if necessary) military toughness. In short, a robust and smart intelligence with some experience of life counted for more than an intense spirituality, scholarly education, or caritative generosity, gifts which in that time were more likely to be met at other levels of the church. Pope Alexander IV seems to have meant in the case of Albert that the theological reputation he had attained would increase his authority as would recent events in Cologne.

Dominican and Professor as Bishop.

Attempts in scholarly research up to the present time to find the great theologian and his writings present in the activities of his episcopal office in Regensburg have not gotten very far. Mainly one document from April 9, 1260 to the Cistercians of Waldsassen is cited.[43] There previously granted indulgences are confirmed and new ones are granted, but there is a sharp command against entrusting that document to wandering preachers who collected money (*"questiarii"*).[44] That abuse Albert had condemned years earlier in

---

of Cologne, Konrad (L. Ennen and G. Eckertz eds., *Quellen zur Geschichte der Stadt Köln* 2 [Cologne, 1863] 423f., Nr. 406; see Scheeben, *Albert* 54.

[42] See H. Hürten, "Die Verbindung von geistlicher und weltlicher Gewalt als Problem in der Amtsführung des mittelalterlichen deutschen Bischofs," *Zeitschrift für Kirchengeschichte* 82 (1971): 16-28; H. Stehkämper, "Der Reichsbishof und Territorialfürst (12. und 13. Jahrhundert)," P. Berglar and O. Engels, eds., *Der Bischof in seiner Zeit. Festgabe für Joseph Kardinal Höffner* (Cologne, 1986) 95-184; W. Janssen, "Der Bischof, Reichsfürst und Landesherr (14. und 15. Jahrhundert)," *Bischof in seiner Zeit* 185-244.

[43] In the view of Staber, *Albertus* 190f.; Mai, *Albertus* 31.

[44] See Mai, *Urkunden* 15: "...*firmiter inhibentes, ne dicte littere per questiarios deportentur et, si secus actum fuerit, decernimus ipsas litteras extunc minime valituras.*"

general terms in his commentary on Peter Lombard's *Sentences*.[45] If one can find here and there some heightened resonance between his personal theological positions and his determinations as bishop, still, it must have been clear to Albert from the beginning that Regensburg did not need an intellectual teacher and researcher. Neither from the papal letter of nomination nor from any other statement in this connection can one extract a sense that bishops as such had an exceptional share in the teaching authority of the church. Similarly, it is difficult to support the view that Albert's elevation is to be understood as an attitude of approval towards his mode of theological thinking or that it was understood by him in this way.[46] In fact, leading and productive theologians were at that time no longer bishops (this had been different in the era of the fathers of the church or in the Carolingian period leading to a figure like Anselm of Canterbury).[47] The professionalization of the academic enterprise in the twelfth century and the development of the bishop as a ruler led to two forms of existence quite distinct from each other. Albert's path to Regensburg was for that time totally untypical, a crossing of boundaries – and that stage lasted briefly.

A second, no less important crossing of boundaries resulted from the fact that Albertus Magnus at the time when he assumed the episcopal see of Regensburg had belonged for more than three decades[48] to the

---

[45] "*Limitatio rationabilis est propter nimium abusum indulgentiarum, quae modo fiunt,*" a text from *Super IV Sententiarum*, d. 20, a. 21 from the later 1240s (Borgnet edition, vol. 29 [Paris, 1894] 858a). A clearer critique of "*quaestiarii*" is found in the *Liber de muliere forti seu In cap. XI Proverbiorum* 15, 1; vol. 18 (Paris: Vivès, 1893) 111b. But there is a question whether this text, if it is even authentic, does not come from 1264/67, that is after the Regensburg episcopacy; see H. Lauer, *Die Moraltheologie Alberts des Grossen mit besonderer_Berücksichtigung ihrer Beziehungen zur Lehre des hl. Thomas* (Freiburg, 1911) 332f.

[46] Scheeben *Albert* 56; Staber, *Albertus* 189.

[47] For this period there is no study analogous to R. Weigand, "Frühe Kanonisten und ihre Karriere in der Kirche," *Zeitschrift der Savigny-Stiftung für Rechtsgeschichte, Kanonistische Abteilung* 76 (1990): 135-155 from which we learn that it was relatively easier for important canonists of the twelfth and thirteenth century to become bishops.

[48] On the uncertain dating of his entry into the Order see Scheeben, *Albert* 8ff.

Order of Preachers of St. Dominic.[49] At that time it was already a community of thousands, a community like that of the friars minor of St. Francis who followed Christ in conscious renunciation of every material security and thereby stood apart from the great mass of the laity but also from the clergy and older monastic orders supported by land and endowments.[50] The Dominican Order, to succeed in the ministries it had chosen like religious education and combating heresy by means of scientific study, developed its own hierarchy and its own territorial structures existing alongside the ordinary constitutional structure of the church. The Order of Preachers found its legal support in the privileges granted it by the central authority of the papacy.[51] The tensions, and even open conflict, that arose from those parallel forms of ecclesial hierarchy and mendicant friars cannot be presented here nor can the ambivalent attitude of men and women of that time whose attitude towards the ascetic and pastoral presence of the Dominicans ranged from enthusiastic admiration to spiteful criticism.

What is important in connection with Albert is that the episcopacy to some extent seemed to run against the inner logic of the mendicant orders (and so the position of the Dominicans), although a few friars had accepted that office in the regular hierarchy of the church.[52] The

---

[49] See A. Vauchez, "Die Bettelorden und ihr Wirken in der städtischen Gesellschaft," A. Vauchez, ed., *Machtfülle des Papsttums (1054-1274)* (Freiburg, 1994) 837ff; L. Canetti, "Intorno all' "idolo delle origini": la storia dei primi frati Predicatori," *I frati Predicatori nel Duecento* (Verona, 1996) 9-51.

[50] See M.-H. Vicaire, "Les origines de la pauvreté mendiante des prêcheurs," M. H. Vicaire, ed., *Dominique et ses prêcheurs* (Fribourg, 1977) 222-265; M. Mollat, *Die Armen im Mittelalter* (Munich, 1984) 108ff.

[51] See Y. M-J. Congar, "Aspects ecclésiologiques de la querelle entre mendiants et séculiers dans la seconde moitié du XIIIe siècle et le début du XIVe," *Archives d'histoire doctrinale et littéraire du moyen âge,"* 36 (1961): 35-51; J. Miethke, "Politische Theorie und die 'Mentalität' der Bettelorden," F. Graus, ed., *Mentalitäten im Mittelalter. Methodische und inhaltliche Probleme* (Sigmaringen, 1987) 157-176.

[52] See P. R. Oliger, *Les évêques réguliers. Recherche sur leur condition juridique depuis les origines du monachisme jusqu' à la fin du moyen-âge* (Paris, 1958) 127ff.; W. R. Thomson, *Friars in the Cathedral. The First Franciscan Bishops 1226-1261* (Toronto, 1975) 9ff.

old monastic reserve toward any ecclesiastical ambition had kept
Benedict of Nursia, Benedict of Aniane, the great abbots of Cluny, and
even Bernard of Clairvaux from accepting episcopal consecration. For
the mendicants in the thirteenth century there was also the conviction
that the existential condition of being a bishop led to the exact
opposite of a life of voluntary poverty – and not just in Germany where
normally the episcopacy was linked to noble rank.[53] Thomas of Celano,
the biographer of St. Francis, reports (or constructs) the anecdote of a
conversation of Cardinal Hugolin with Francis and Dominic. There the
future pope describes the early church where the spiritual shepherds
were poor and were men full of the love of neighbor, and not desirous
of money and position (*"pauperes erant et homines caritate, non
cupiditate ferventes"*). So now the brothers in the new orders should be
made bishops to give others a visible example (*"qui documento et
exemplo caeteris praevalent"*). Dominic immediately rejects this with
the words: "Rightly understood my brothers are already raised to high
rank, and I, to the extent that I have anything to say about it, will not
allow them to accept any further kind of dignity" (*"nec pro meo posse
permittam, ut aliud assequantur specimen dignitatis"*).[54]

That was not to be the last word on this topic. The general chapters
of the Dominicans stated many times between 1234 and 1255 their
decision that no friar could become a bishop without the previous

---

[53] Stephanus de Salaniaco et Bernardus Guidonis, *De quatuor in quibus deus
Praedicatorum Ordinem insignivit* III 5, 259, T. Kaeppeli ed. (Rome, 1949) 118;
see M. H. Vicaire, *Geschichte des heiligen Dominikus* 1 (Freiburg, 1962) 196f.;
Staber, *Albertus* 179.

[54] Thomas of Celano, *Vita secunda S. Francisci* ch. 109 (148) in *Legendae S.
Francisci Assisiensis saeculis XIII et XIV conscriptae* I (Quaracchi-Firenze, 1926-
1941) 215f.; see B. Altaner, "Die Beziehungen des hl. Dominikus zum hl.
Franziskus von Assisi," *Franziskanische Studien* 9 (1922): 1-28, particularly
22; Oliger, *Les évêques* 134f.; K. Elm, "Franziskus und Dominikus. Wirkungen
und Antriebskräfte zweier Ordensstifter," *Saeculum* 23 (1972): 127-147;
Elm's article is reprinted in D. Berg, ed., *Vitasfratrum. Beiträge zur Geschichte
der Eremiten- und Mendikantenorden des zwölften und__dreizehnten
Jahrhunderts* (Werl, 1994) 121-141.

permission of the master of the Order or the provincial,[55] although that reservation took into account the actual development, namely, that the first Dominican bishops had been appointed already from the second half of the 1220s. The earliest documented cases of Dominican bishops[56] are to be found in Morocco, the Balkans, and Finland: they can be said to be in harmony with the discipline of the Order because they result directly from missionary work in countries without a fixed hierarchy.[57] So from the 1230s to the 1250s bishops who are Dominicans come from boarder areas of Latin Christianity where the office is hardly a prize for the ambitious and where it does not bring the disrepute of abandoning an ideal of personal poverty. Nonetheless, there are also a few Dominicans at that time among bishops in northern and central Italy, and in southern France and Spain[58]; that is, in the areas where the Order was most numerous. In 1260, as Albert was given this office, there was already a Dominican who was a cardinal: Hugh of Saint-Cher was created a cardinal in 1244.[59] There had already been two friars in Germany who wore the miter. Heinrich I

---

[55] B. M. Reichert, *Acta capitulorum generalium Ordinis Praedicatorum* 1 (Rome-Stuttgart, 1898): 4 (1233); 61 (1252); 67 (1254); 72 (1255); see Scheeben, *Albert* 55; Oliger, *Les évêques* 153.

[56] Literature in this area depends on G. Gumbley, "Series praesulum assumptorum ex Ord. Praed.," *Analecta sacri Ordinis fratrum Praedicatorum* 17 (1925): 577-586, 649f., 767-778: up until 1319 and in particulars undependable (the two earliest references for 1221 and 1224 are at any rate to be set aside); see R. Schieffer, "Die frühesten Bischöfe aus dem Dominikanerorden," Franz J. Felten, Nikolas Jaspert, Stephanie Haarländer, eds., *Vita Religiosa im Mittelalter* (Berlin, 1999) 405-419.

[57]See. B. Altaner, *Die Dominikanermissionen des 13. Jahrhunderts. Forschungen zur Geschichte der kirchlichen Unionen und der Mohammedaner- und Heidenmission des Mittelalters* (Habelschwerdt, 1924).

[58] A particular case is Guala de Roniis, prior of the Dominican priory in Brescia, raised to the episcopacy of that city by Gregory IX in 1229/30; see C. Violante, "La chiesa bresciana nel medioevo," *Storia di Brescia* 1 (Brescia, 1963) 1001-1124, particularly 1077f.

[59] See J. H. H. Sassen, *Hugo von St. Cher. Seine Tätigkeit als Kardinal 1244 - 1263* (Bonn, 1908).

of Chiemsee[60] was bishop after 1252 but because of the odd legal position of this diocese he was not an imperial prince and was given his position by the Archbishop of Salzburg. A second case was Henry III of Chur.[61] He had been previously a Dominican papal penitentiary, but as a member of the noble house of Montfort dominating the region he was in 1252 canonically chosen by the cathedral chapter to be bishop. Struggling against the nobility of that diocese, he avoided for seventeen years episcopal consecration until 1268.[62]

Against this background one understands better how the raising of the Dominican Albert to the see of Regensburg was for the German situation no utterly unheard of act. Still, because of the importance of the diocese and the prominence of the man elevated, it found considerable attention in and outside the Order. Some deeply rooted reservations against this kind of promotion again became vocal. To express them fell, because of his office, to the Master of the Order, Humbert of Romans.[63] He was the fourth successor to St. Dominic as the leader of the Friars Preachers and was personally well acquainted with Albert. In an emotional letter,[64] whose retention and subsequent transmission is in more than one aspect remarkable,[65] he, as soon as

---

[60] See E. Wallner, *Das Bistum Chiemsee im Mittelalter (1215-1508)* (Rosenheim, 1967) 92ff.

[61] See O. P. Clavadetscher, W. Kundert, "Das Bistum Chur," A. Bruckner ed., *Helvetia Sacra* I/I (Bern, 1972) 480.

[62] See B. Bilgeri, *Geschichte Vorarlbergs 1: Vom freien Rätien zum Staat der Montforter* (Vienna, 1971) 170ff.

[63] See D.-A. Mortier, *Histoire des maîtres généraux de l'Ordre des frères prêcheurs* 1 (Paris, 1903) 445-664; F. Heintke, *Humbert von Romans, der fünfte Ordensmeister der Dominikaner* (Berlin, 1933).

[64] Printed in Scheeben, *Albert* 154ff. Nr. 25; see Mortier, *Histoire* 646ff.; Oliger, *Évêques* 188f.; Staber, *Albertus* 178ff.

[65] The textual tradition used by Scheeben's *Albert* is in accord with the brief biography by Ludwig of Valladolid from around 1414; see also H. C. Scheeben, "Die Tabulae Ludwigs von Valladolid im Chor der Predigerbrüder von St. Jakob in Paris," *Archivum Fratrum Praedicatorum* 1 (1931): 223-263, particularly 229.

he heard the first rumors circulating in the Curia concerning the possible elevation of Albert, put pressure on the friar and "*lector Coloniensis*" to refuse. His letter asks: Does he, at the end of his life, want to stain (Humbert refers to the office of bishop as "*maculam huiusmodi*") his reputation and that of the Order? Every layperson ("*secularis*") who hears about this will be shocked at Albert and at all the others in the religious state; they will think that we – the mendicants – do not love poverty but only put up with it until we can get beyond it. His superior warns Albert directly about making a decision based on his annoyance at certain difficulties in the Order ("*alique molestie ordinis*") encountered by him, or about simply yielding to papal directives, for experience shows that if you resist them decisively enough ("*aliquem volentem efficaciter resistere*") compliance will not be forced. Even more, Albert should keep before his eyes what has happened to those who let themselves be drawn into something like the office of bishop (apparently nothing good!) and what difficulties would lie ahead of him precisely in Germany ("*in regimine ecclesiarum in Teutonia*"), and what risks to the health of the soul lie amid secular business and other dangers of sin. Humbert's letter ends with the emotional call: "I would rather hear that my beloved son lies in his coffin then that he sits on the bishop's chair."

A direct answer from Albert to this serious challenge has not come down to us. His de facto response was that he accepted the higher position – beyond the reservations of the superior of the Order and in line with the papal decree. He did not agonize over his decision very long, for the letter of appointment by Pope Alexander from Anagni issued on January 5, 1260 reached him in Cologne where documents place him on January 23d and March 1st,[66] and in the course of March he is in Würzburg on the way to Regensburg.[67] Whether informal contacts with the Curia or a prior questionnaire gave Albert an earlier opportunity to think about his own stance is completely uncertain[68] as is the time when the opposing view of the Master of the Order reached him, a text in which Regensburg is not expressly stated but mention is made only of general plans for making Albert a bishop. Humbert of

---

[66] See Stehkämper, *Pro bono pacis* 308ff., Nr. 5-7.

[67] See note 3 in this article.

[68] Scheeben rightly has doubts about this (*Albert* 54).

Romans himself, however, was true to his views, for two years later he refused the offer of Pope Urban IV to become Patriarch of Jerusalem and after stepping down from leading the Order went back to Lyons to live as an ordinary Dominican.[69] In a different existence, Albert lived long enough to experience in 1276 a Dominican friar accepting even election to the papacy, although the pontificate of Innocent V lasted only five months.[70] To what extent Albert, after accepting the episcopal office, sought to live in a Dominican way is unknown. It is worth noting that during his Regensburg period in almost all documents he as a member of his Order placed *"frater"* before his name,[71] although not one of those documents brings any special benefit to the local priory of the Dominicans at the church of St. Blase.[72]

An Early Resignation.

In contrast to Albert's elevation to the episcopacy his resignation after two years is only slightly documented. The fact is clear from the circular letter (already mentioned) of Urban IV from May 11, 1262, confirming his successor Leo; in a few formalistic phrases it mentions the resignation of Albert which the Pope accepted after consulting those around him.[73] Reasons for the resignation are not mentioned; nor, as far as I can see, did Albert ever mention them in later years. We have no documented criticism of him either from Regensburg or from anywhere else. There is no doubt about continuing contacts between Albert and Urban IV, for the Pope after a further period spent by Albert

---

[69] See Heintke 78f. Certainly the offer cannot first have been made in 1263; see Stephanus de Salaniaco et Bernardus Guidonis, *De quatuor...*, 118, line 22.

[70] See M.-H. Laurent, *Le bienheureux Innocent V (Pierre de Tarantaise) et son temps* (Città del Vaticano, 1947), particularly 107ff.

[71] See Mai, *Urkunden* 10.

[72] See M. Popp, "Die Dominikaner im Bistum Regensburg," G. Schwaiger, P. Mai, eds., *Klöster und Orden im Bistum Regensburg. Beiträge zu ihrer Geschichte* (Regensburg, 1978) 227-257, particularly 232.

[73] Ried, *Codex* 465: "...per cessionem venerabilis fratris nostri Alberti episcopi quondam Ratisponensis ab eo petitam instanter et tandem de consilio fratrum nostrorum a nobis admissam..."

at the Curia named him on February 13, 1263, preacher for the crusade in Germany, Bohemia, and other German-speaking areas. [74] Many documents in the following years introduce him as "*frater Albertus*" and at the same time "*episcopus quondam Ratisponensis,*" [75] and similarly documents of his Dominican brothers when they speak of him mention his episcopal rank.[76]

Albert by laying down the shepherd's crosier of Regensburg did not lose the sacramentally grounded dignity of being bishop nor did he simply become again a Dominican like the other friars. This is particularly clear from his will and testament of January, 1279.[77] He listed the priory of friars preachers in Cologne as the beneficiary of his books, his vestments, and his objects made of gold, silver, and pearls; he commissioned representatives to see that financial contributions reach the Dominican nuns in Würzburg, Augsburg and (Schwäbisch) Gmünd. He expressly asked that with his money ("*de pecunia mea*") the choir section of the Order's church in Cologne dedicated to the Holy Cross be brought to completion, and this thanks to his will his confreres were able to do. To dispose of goods, to have had income was for the author of the testament introducing himself at the beginning of the document as "*frater Albertus episcopus quondam Ratisponensis ordinis fratrum Praedicatorum*" not completely without difficulty, and so in a kind of preamble he emphasized his right to personal property as something exceptional in the Order and given to him by the pope ("*ratione exemptionis ab ordine a summo pontifice*

---

[74] The respective documents are published in J. Guiraud, *Les registres d'Urbain IV (1261 - 1264)* 1 (Paris, 1901) 86, Nr. 311; see Potthast, *Regesta*, Nr. 18491; V. Cramer, *Albert der Grosse als Kreuzzugs-Legat für Deutschland 1263/64 und die Kreuzzugs-Bestrebungen Urbans IV* (Cologne, 1933).

[75] See Scheeben, *Albert* 138ff., Nr. 3-14, 17, 21, 24 (for the years from 1263 to 1276).

[76] Examples can be found in H. Finke, *Ungedruckte Dominikaner-briefe des 13. Jahrhunderts* (Paderborn, 1891) 84f., Nrs. 53 and 55.

[77] Published in J. A. Schmeller, "Über einige minder bekannte kleinere Textstücke aus den Handschriften der k. Hof- und Staatsbibliothek," *Gelehrte Anzeigen* 30 (1850): 34-47, particularly 45ff.; see G.M. Löhr, *Beiträge zur Geschichte des Kölner Dominikanerklosters im Mittelalter* II (Leipzig, 1922) 32f., Nr. 58; see Scheeben, *Albert* 123 on the dating.

mihi facte").[78] Without doubt this particular status was linked to being a bishop; the "*exemptio ab ordine*" certainly meant not only private ownership but an extensive liberation from the discipline ("*obedientia*") of the Order, an aspect of religious life quite difficult to harmonize with the exercise of the episcopal office. Since the ensemble of these aspects of his life emerged more or less already in 1260 with Albert's call to Regensburg, one should conclude that the "*exemptio ab ordine*" as a papal privilege mentioned by Albert in his will refers to arrangements made at the time of his resignation in 1262. It gave him, no longer a bishop of a diocese, a special position in and amid the Order of Preachers and included the right to private income. Moreover, after 1262 he assumed no more positions of leadership in the Order, unlike the situation before 1260.

This throws some light on the tension between Albert and Humbert, the Master of the Order, at the beginning of the year 1260. Both would have been aware that the step which the Pope planned would be irreversible and would have consequences for the entire Order. What Humbert sought to block Albert seems precisely to have sought: a special position legitimated by the papacy, a position vis-à-vis certain enmities within the Dominicans, namely the "alique molestie ordinis" who sought to reduce the influence of such a prominent personality. That kind of position would give to the great theologian through the episcopacy more freedom than would normally be possible. If the peaceful resolution of the situation in Regensburg was the explicit motivating reason for the pope who named him, nonetheless, Albert might have seen that enterprise as a beginning. Quite soon he sized up being a mediator there as a temporarily limited role but also saw it at the same time as a benefit which over time would bring him a special effect, "*exemptio ab ordine.*" When two years later a harmonious election to the bishopric was again possible in Regensburg, he turned at once to other enterprises and left further developments on the Danube to men from that city and region.

Thirteenth Century Sources and Later Legends.

We could at this point bring this essay to a conclusion except that some sources hand on further information, clarifying or illuminating

---

[78] See particularly Scheeben, *Albert* 123ff. ; Oliger, *Évêques* 194.

data, which experts in studies on Albert the Great would have missed in the previous presentation. These details, not mentioned up to this point in this essay, are found in narrative sources from the time after Albert's death, in various drafts of the so-called Albert-Legend which in its fully developed form exists only from the end of the fourteenth century but naturally had various prior stages.[79] What those stories offer for a portrait of Albert's life stands at times in clear opposition to the facts that can be drawn from documents and letters of the thirteenth century, and to that extent they deserve no trust. To a very large extent they are reports that elude close examination and consequently have experienced only slight scientific evaluation. Mentioning them at the end of this essay on material treating Albert's time as bishop of Regensburg does not aim at debating the value of each of these sources but rather at noting that those later descriptions of Albert, mainly from Dominican writers and always intent upon giving an edifying portrait, were fashioned according to the pattern of a stylized hero in terms of the ideal of the Order as pictured for the time of Albert. So indirectly they do illumine the discrepancies appearing at the center of this essay.

Their repeated insistence that Albert accepted the bishop's crosier only through force and against all kinds of objections on his part is understandable,[80] and his presence at the Curia at the time of his nomination is asserted in order to give him the possibility of immediately presenting his objections.[81] Since, in fact, contemporary documents offer nothing that points to any hesitation on the part of

---

[79] See de Loë, *De Vita* 19, 257ff.; F. Pelster, *Kritische Studien zum Leben und zu den Schriften Alberts des Grossen* (Freiburg, 1920), 1 ff.; Scheeben, *Albert* 1ff.; W. P. Eckert, "Albert-Legenden," A. Zimmerman, ed., *Albert der Grosse. Seine Zeit, sein Werk, seine Wirkung* (Berlin, 1981) 1-23. For the state of research on sources up to 1500, see Schieffer, "Übersicht der biographischen Quellen über Albert (sog. Albert-Legende) bis 1500," published as an "Anhang" to that article (*Lectio Albertina* 3, 21-25).

[80] Stephanus de Salaniaco et Bernardus Guidonis, *De quatuor...*III 5, 167 and 77: "Episcopatum Ratisponensem coactus accepit," in de Loë, "Legenda Coloniensis" ch. 11 in *De Vita* 19, 275; "ipsum *plurimum renitentem.*" For supporting documents see texts in Scheeben, *Albert* 54f.

[81] De Loë, "Legenda Coloniensis," ch. 11 in *De Vita* 19, 275.

the Cologne professor toward the plan of Alexander IV, in later legends there is less and less of imagining what might be Albert's motives; the remaining hesitation is the traditional monastic reserve toward high church offices, something overcome by the Dominican's pride in the papal preference given to his Order. Similarly one edifying narrative treats the problem of how to reconcile mendicancy with episcopal dignity by narrating how Albert modestly avoided a solemn entry into Regensburg and spent the evening of his arrival with the Dominicans at St. Blase who led him the next day to visit his cathedral for the first time.[82] With some probability, the introduction of the feast of Dominic in the calendar of saints in the Regensburg church can be ascribed to him,[83] while one should view more skeptically the frequent mention of his simple sandals leaving behind among people a memory of his poverty.[84] In terms of important events in his episcopal activity later reports fashion different ideal images: for instance, he used all the time he could find to withdraw to the episcopal residence at Burg Donaustauf to compose there, within a year, his commentary on the Gospel according to Luke,[85] or through clever economics he applied

---

[82] Ibid.; Scheeben, *Albert* 58f.

[83] Petrus von Preussen, *Legenda Alberti Magni* ch. 36 (a text printed in Cologne in 1483 (see W.A. Copinger, *Supplement to Hain's Repertorium Bibliographicum. Or, Collections towards a new editions of that work* (London 1895-1902), 1 Nr. 4443. fol. 70'); see Scheeben, *Albert* 62f.

[84] Andreas von Regensburg, *Chronica pontificum et imperatorum Romanorum ad a. 1260* edited by G. Leidinger (Munich, 1903) 66; Scheeben, *Albert* 62.

[85] De Loë, "Legenda Coloniensis," ch. 13 in *De Vita* 19, 276; with the designation of a *"castrum super Danubium situm"* (Rudolphus de Novimagio, *Legenda litteralis Alberti Magni* book 2, c. 3 (text printed in Cologne in 1490, in Ludovicus Hain, *Repertorium bibliographicum: in quo libri omnes ab arte typographica inventa usque ad annum MD. typis expressi, ordine alphabetico vel simpliciter enumerantur vel adcuratius recensentur* (Lutetiae Parisiorum [Paris],1826-1838) [reprint Staten Island: Maurizio Matino, 1996].11915, fol 19, with the identification of that place as (Donau-) Stauf; this is the view too of Laurentius Hochwart, *Catalogus episcoporum Ratisponensium*, bk. 3, ch. 9 in the edition of A. F. Oefele, *Rerum Boicarum Scriptores* 1 (Augustae Vindelicorum [Augsburg] 1763) 207; see Scheeben, *Albert* 62. These may be linked to Albert himself who in his *De animalibus* 7, tr. 2, c. 6 (in the edition of H. Stadler [Münster, 1916] 523) writes of observing nature "in villa mea super Danubium." Moreover the Dominican priory in Regensburg according

four hundred and eighty six pounds of silver to diocesan debts, rectifying the finances of the diocese.[86] And the reason for the resignation – writers like to link it to an earlier forced acceptance of the office – falls usually into the framework that he wanted to return home to the poverty of his Order![87] Sources in the following two centuries find three other possible motivations for the resignation: humility before a pastoral assignment of such breadth, rapid exhaustion after first attempts to master the amount of work,[88] or disappointment in finding himself dealing with a diocese where people were stubborn and intractable.[89] Or too, he had a deep dislike of the usual military aspects of being a prince of the empire, even a prince in the spiritual realm.[90] Finally there is his lasting preference for scholarly work.[91] All of these – and many others imagined by modern biographers to support their explanations – cannot be sustained (even less can they be contradicted) by Albert's own statements. In the last analysis, these are simply attempts to answer the kinds of questions

---

to the catalogue of their library in 1347 had a copy of the commentary on Luke; see C. E. Ineichen-Eder, *Mittelalterliche Bibliothekskataloge Deutschlands und der Schweiz IV/I: Bistümer Passau und Regensburg* (Munich, 1977) 456, 41.

[86] Documents supporting this idea are cited in the sixteenth century; Hochwart, *Catalogus* 207; Scheeben, *Albert* 59; Mai, *Albertus* 31.

[87] Stephanus de Salaniaco et Bernardus Guidonis, *De quatuor* ...III 5, 167: "*quem paulo post tanquam carbonem ardentem manum adurentem obtenta cessione reiecit...et ad ordinis rediit paupertatem.*" 97.

[88] Hermann von Niederaltaich, *Annales ad a. 1261* in *MGH SS* 17, 402; Heinrich von Herford, *Liber de rebus memorabilibus sive Chronicon ad a. 1266* A. Potthast, ed. (Göttingen, 1859) 201; see Scheeben, *Albert* 63f.

[89] Andreas von Regensburg, *Chronica pontificum et imperatorum Romanorum ad a. 1260* 66; Hochwart, *Catalogus* 208; Scheeben, *Albert* 63f.

[90] Tholomaeus von Lucca, *Historia ecclesiastica* bk. 22, ch. 19 cited in L. A. Muratori, ed., *Rerum Italicarum scriptores* 11 (Mediolani [Milan], 1727), column 1151; Scheeben, *Albert* 64.

[91] Petrus von Preussen, *Legenda Alberti Magni* ch. 37 (folio 70 verso); see Staber, Albertus 192 and note 105. [The original text of the article here translated has an "*Anhang*" giving bibliographical information concerning twelve basic texts on Albert's life.]

that the events themselves raise for observers, then as today, events that do not explain themselves.

At the end of this discussion it is worthwhile asking why a closer look at this episode in Albert's life is important. Certainly not for a better understanding of his theological and philosophical works which in their totality hold almost no autobiographical references and mirror an intellectual development largely detached from any connection to particular places. Rather it is important for every interpretation to grasp that Albert steps before us (in contrast to Thomas Aquinas) as a writer who did not go through life exclusively as a scholar, but who in the Order, in the society around him, and in the church took on offices and positions with practical dimensions among which the exercise for a while of the episcopacy at Regensburg is only the most prominent. In his contact with that bishopric there is a remarkable measure of self-consciousness and preparedness for conflict in light of the norms of the Order, the wishes of the papacy, and the needs of the diocese entrusted to him. That we are able to deepen our view of the tensions connected with that episcopacy depends on a tradition of information sustained and furthered by the importance given to the great theologian. That information permits us to study in this individual case, one well presented in documentary sources, the visible tensions between professional theology, defined religious groups, and hierarchical order which have formed the being of the church, at that time in the thirteenth century – but not only then.

Hugo Stehkämper

Albertus Magnus and the Cologne Reconciliation of April 17, 1271

Albert was someone who labored for Cologne and for the welfare of Cologne, and he was well known for those efforts, an enterprise quite removed from academic scholarship. During his lifetime he took part in at least twenty-five mediations seeking peace between contesting groups: five of these concerned the city of Cologne. It says a great deal that this city called him in those times of crisis to join the commission set up for settling a dispute (at that time the parties in conflict decided on the mediators).

Albert who had been living and working in Strassburg for some years (apparently from 1267) received at the end of 1270 from the Master of the Dominicans John of Vercelli an agitated letter. "I ask you, I beg you to stay with your useful plan for the friars: namely to remain with your desired and necessary intention to go to Cologne, for the clergy of that city long for and demand your presence. There the streams of the holy fountain entrusted to you can be useful in various ways to many, to both the friars and others." Albert intended after receiving this letter to go at once to Cologne, but then he changed his mind. The reason for this change of mind certainly came first of all from the situation in Cologne: a devastating conflict had broken out between the city and the Archbishop Engelbert von Falkenburg (1261-1274), the successor to Konrad von Hochstaden, for which there seemed no way out. The new Archbishop had involved himself in various deceptions and in the breaking of agreements, and so the city turned again to violence and to the disregard of ecclesiastical penalties. Each attempt at even beginning to seek some possibility of peace between the two parties seemed doomed.

Earlier Konrad von Hochstaden had pursued conflict on many fronts. He was not content with the rights given him by the Great Decision of Cologne in 1252. Egotism, extravagance, simony, arbitrary decisions, venality, and nepotism were behind his decision in April, 1259 (supported by the majority of the population) to remove from a role in trials the permanent jurors and to replace them with persons not of the nobility. To support those measures Konrad argued from the document of conciliation accepted just a year before. In fact, that text gave him no such right. The constitution of the city was actually strengthened by that agreement, and now the next Archbishop had thrown it out. That was a revolution from above.

The new city officials whom he had just solemnly recognized were offended. His entry into Cologne on June 8, 1262 with an army was a clear action against them. He occupied all the city gates and walls with his troops and turned the Riehler and Bayen towers into fortresses. In short, the city began to be the site of a military chess match. Never before had an archbishop risked that kind of aggression. Further, he required that the income of the city from the mills, basic taxes, tolls, and taxes on beer become his own revenues. He fired the jurors which the upper classes had selected and notified them that he would replace them with others. Moreover, he intended to supervise the nobility through an official and a mayor named by him.

Konrad von Hochstaden despite his own desire for military supervision had given to the city a militia (mustered up by him) and this kept the appearance of independence. Now Engelbert wanted full subjection to him, a subjection extending to the other cities of the Archdiocese. He had gone too far. Without taking notice of the newly appointed city leaders the civic community he called the noble families to assemble outside the city, and on that very day, June 8th, in a hard fought battle conquered the troops of the Archbishop. The city made financial concessions, while the Archbishop agreed to give it the independence for which it had fought. The "Great Agreement" of 1252 was to be the model for a permanent arrangement, and everything that happened after its signing, whether documented or not, was declared null and void. The noble families received back their traditional rights and offices. Consequently the Archbishop continued the city militia as made up of soldiers of noblebirth.

The Archbishop, however, was not stopped by this defeat. Bitter and determined, he fought on with violent attacks behind the scenes to extend his dominance of the city. Up to the end of 1265 he agreed to four further processes taking place aiming at reconciliation. He would, however, at once break the solemn agreements he had promised because they required him to make further concessions in tariffs and legal procedures. In the area around Cologne trust in him faded, as he ceaselessly stirred up divisions among the population. The guilds sought to overthrow the nobles in 1264 and 1265 but failed; the Overstolzen defeated them in 1267 and stopped the Muhlengasse-Weisen supported by Engelbert in 1268. Through the involvement of his brother Dietrich (a military captain who eventually died in these conflicts) as well as the complicity of the highly respectable Weisen family linked to him Engelbert became the instigator of a risky military enterprise on the Ulre gate in the night of October 14th, 1268.

Moreover, the Archbishop sought to use church penalties to achieve his goals. Engelbert in November, 1263 during a session of his court lied to the citizenry about his views on increasing his power. They, aware of his deceptions, seized him in his palace, and held him for twenty days in the House *"Zum Ross"* in the Rheingasse. He reacted by extending the excommunication pronounced on those taking part in his capture to an interdict covering the entire city. He used diocesan statues from May 10th, 1266, to excommunicate all the citizens of Cologne as well as Count Wilhelm von Jülich. The view that those allied against the Archbishop could not attain salvation only intensified their activities. Count Wilhelm on October 18th, 1267, captured the Archbishop in the battle of Marienholz near Zülpich -- the Archbishop was in full armor with a sword in his hand -- and imprisoned him in the Nideggen castle. Pope Clement IV in 1268 sent a nuntius, Bernhard of Castaneto, but he did not serve as a true mediator and sided with the Archbishop. He avoided Cologne which was joined to the Jülich party, and on August 1268 he forbade there any celebration of Mass, the administration of a sacrament, or any pastoral activity whatsoever. The city immediately appealed to the pope. The pope, however, died on November 29th, 1268, and it was only three years later on September 1st, 1271, that the cardinals could agree on a successor. Meanwhile, Castaneto's interdict was not always strictly observed, for his behavior did not please the clergy in Cologne. The Nuntius intensified his measures and commanded all diocesan priests to leave the city within two months and not to return until the Archbishop was set free. The clergy saw the seriousness of the situation. Castaneto forbade any commerce among the citizens, something causing great difficulty for the city. If their first appeal to the pope had not had any results, it was foreseeable that the two protests against an even stricter procedure of the Nuntius would have no effect – and there was in fact no pope to receive an appeal.

Rigidity and the desire for revenge had replaced the will to find an end to this war of some years. This was the situation when the letter from the Master of the Dominicans cited above reached Albert asking him to go to Cologne, even as Albert had come to see the situation as not promising. The Dominicans' view was that Albert's presence was important and that the diocesan clergy in Cologne "longed" for him. Albert would have seen in those words in the letter that serious problems were making life in Cologne difficult. No Mass could be celebrated in the city, and no one could be baptized, married or buried; for most people the means of salvation given by the church were not accessible. The city, nonetheless, sought to bypass the interdict by paying priests who came from elsewhere to perform the liturgy. Albert's conviction that there was no way out of this political situation kept him away from Cologne. Still, when his fellow Dominicans described to him the spiritual situation of the people in detail, he decided to go. Thus it was that Albert as a pastorally concerned person undertook to resolve a situation which seemed to him politically incapable of resolution.

The key to peace lay, first and foremost, in the hands of Archbishop Engelbert. Often conquered but still striving in a rigid way to subject Cologne to himself he was accused by the important clergy and the city's cathedral chapter as well as by much of the diocese as someone guilty of fracturing peace. However, he seemed to have had little awareness of his total lack of success. Humiliated by imprisonment for three and a half years and made bitter by the death of his brother, he had neither the will nor the strength to free himself from all these intrigues.

If we can trust Gottfried Hagen – he had composed his chronicle a year after these events (the precise words attributed to Albert by Gottfried are certainly not his) – Albert spoke to the Archbishop in a way that forcefully challenged his decisions from the point of view of his conscience. The scenario that when Engelbert met with Albert he was full of remorse is certainly an invention. Nonetheless, it seems true that Albert spoke freely to Falkenburg about reconciliation with the city of Cologne. The Reconciliation of April 17, 1271, permits us to see how Albert brought peace about. The city prevailed in political and commercial areas. There was a direct proclamation that was not simply the result of compromise; the tone implied that Engelbert conceded that his entire style of ruling up to that point was a failure. Certain formulations in the act of reconciliation attract one's notice: for instance, Engelbert says that "we want that those under our direction to enjoy every peace" and "we recognize that it is given to us to exercise protection and peace and beneficence all the time." Five times Engelbert mentions in a general way the citizens of Cologne but thirty-eight times he refers to "our" citizens. One should remember that in 1226 when Archbishop Heinrich von Müllenmark (1225-1238) designated the people in Cologne as his subjects his document was rejected and a new one without this disturbing description was accepted. In his fifty-three objections to the previous Great Reconciliation Konrad von Hochstaden had not used the words "subject" or "inferior." Here, even when he was being conquered and imprisoned, the proud Falkenberg still said that the Cologne citizens were subjects of him and the archdiocese. Albert made clear to him that the self-understanding of the citizens would reaction to those expressions negatively. One suspects that all this took a great deal of negotiation. The citizens saw themselves as free; their city's freedom was one of their greatest possessions. Expressions implying the opposite would excite a strong reaction. Ultimately Albert used the argument that the ten years in which the city suffered under the interdict with wretched side effects had injured the civil order and the economic condition of the city. This had to be ended. Engelbert interpreted the reconciliation – in fact it was an act of capitulation – as an act of graciousness to the city coming from archiepiscopal privilege. His tone, however, would not have bothered Cologne. What was important was that he agreed not to approach the new pope with any new proposals that might injure the raising of the interdict. (In fact, six months later he set aside all the measures to which he had agreed.)

If the *Lesser Decision* of April 17th, 1252, treated conflict in easily compartmentalized areas of law, the *Great Decision* of June 28th, 1258, regulated basic issues like constitutional questions, economics and the politics of the city and society. These two earlier deliberations were Albert's masterful and creative accomplishment in the area of social jurisprudence. The Reconciliation of 1271, however, was an achievement of a high degree in the area of political negotiations.

Henryk Anzulewicz

The End and Renewal of the World (Matthew 5:18 and 24:35)

When we examine in a critical way our consciousness of tradition and our ties to tradition in terms of an understanding of time, the question naturally arises about what a great thinker like Albert the Great would have to say to us about the duration of time. What would he who is *temporally* far away from us but close to us in terms of his horizon of understanding offer us in terms of interpretating the reality of the world and the idea of time? We limit these pages to one aspect of that reflection: his understanding of the fulfillment of time, of the fulfillment of the totality of the reality of being in time. More precisely, we look at his understanding of the temporal end and renewal of the world in the eternity of God.

In his theological and philosophical writings the *"Doctor universalis"* holds the view that time presents the measure of the movement bringing to completion being under the conditions of contingency, that is, of space and time. They in turn move towards a transcendent goal, a goal above time in the eternity of God, a goal in God itself. The movement of reality taking place in time and space brings being to full realization. If time as the creation of God is limited, space and time will experience their end in the eternity of God. If that movement of the self-realization of creation is going to cease, this means not simply the end of the world but rather the end of the world's existence in contingency. There will be an end for the mode of being of the reality of the world connected to matter, the end of space and time.

The theses of the finitude of the world and of the eternity of this world cannot in Albert's view be proven from the world's finite (or eternal) existence in matter, space, and time.[1] Because he treats human reason as created by God and so as limited in its potentiality for knowing, he seeks support in this question from the more secure realm of revealed truth. Nevertheless, this and the truth of reason do not contradict each other but expand each other. Human reason with its limited capability of knowing is drawn toward God as its origin. Human reason can never render the revelation of God superficial. An

---

[1] See Albertus Magnus, *De homine*, tr. 2, q. 80 a. 1.

interpretation of the world exclusively based upon natural reason (something Albert finds above all in the system of Aristotle) is essentially related to the mode of contingency and remains inside the world. The world unfolds before the trans-temporal transcendence of God which is the origin and goal of humanity and being. For Albert, the world viewed from its transcendent origin and goal has a beginning and an end in terms of the duration of beings. A beginning for the world can be supported by arguments from reason and can be the subject of a philosophical discussion, although it can't be proven. Moreover, an end of the world cannot be established philosophically.

Still, Albert represents even in his philosophical writings a view that the world will end, and he emphasizes there that he is drawing from a higher source of truth than philosophy, namely, from biblical revelation. His philosophical writings do not discuss the question about the end of the world because he cannot assume from rational premises that this world has an end. Nonetheless, he holds in philosophical contexts – as in the exposition of the Aristotelian *Physics*, a writing on this issue which was of basic importance for the philosophy of nature in the ancient philosophers of Greece – that the reality of this world because of the will of its Creator will reach an end and a completion.

The views of philosophers on this theme in antiquity are quite diverse. Albert espouses no philosophical viewpoint but presents the position of biblical faith and revelation. Accordingly the world has a beginning which is at the same time the beginning of time. It will have an end not because this is the consequence of the process of nature with its particular structure but because of a special cause external to the reality of this world. A philosopher, however, does not treat those issues because they come from the realm of faith and theology.[2]

Where do we find in the writings of Albertus Magnus the theological question of time? How does he consider eternity which in his perspective is the principle and the goal of the created, transitory, and perduring reality of the world? How does he explain the end and the completion of this self-realizing world in space and time? Albert treats theologically the question about the end and fulfillment of the reality

---

[2] See Albertus Magnus, *Physica,* l. 8, tr. 1, c. 15.

of the world several times in writings on systematic and biblical theology. We limit our presentation to one of his considerations. It is drawn from a biblical text, from a commentary on the *Gospel according to Matthew*. Explaining the words of *Matthew* 5:18 ("until heaven and earth pass away"), he focuses on their content; he also pays attention to parallel passages in that Gospel (*Matthew* 24: 35), material he develops in an excursus on eschatology. The main idea is that the totality of the reality of being (the heavens and the earth) in their material forms accessible to the senses are transitory, while their foundation – the divine law and the explanatory words of Christ -- retain a permanent validity.

According to Albert this world must have an end and experience a renewal. There is always -- and must be -- a cor-respondence between a locality and the people who live there (in this case, human beings). In its original form the world was complete, and this corresponded to the complete constitution of its inhabitants: the first pair of human beings living before the choice for sin. With the fall of Adam and Eve this integral condition of the world disappeared. Then the world corresponded to the changed condition of human beings who no longer had their original fullness. The fall of human beings brought not only a consequent alteration of the human condition but also a negative reduction of the originally complete condition of all creation. If life in its original condition along with the entire process of nature was first immune from crippling forces, after the fall of the first human beings a qualitative change entered. The world of nature lost its original harmony, an inner and outer harmony permeating the interplay of the dynamic powers of nature. Nature without being guilty of this change had to accept a burdensome wound that contradicted nature's realizations of it activities in an integral way. God arranged that after the sin of the first human pair in terms of the elect, the natural world is also involved. Because the human being realizes itself in space and time and because the person who comes from God and moves towards God in self-realization in space and time is to be divinized, this world is to be renewed in a corresponding way.

With regards to the ways in which the renewal of the world will take place, Albert maintains that there are two things to keep in mind. First, there is the means of renewal or the point of departure from which this renewal takes its course. That is fire. The second aspect essential for the renewal process consists in the goal or limit towards which this process of purification unfolds. The beginning of the process of renewal will therefore be linked to fire. Fire annihilates aspects of creation opposing completion and glorification. The Creator will give to the world a transfigured form: he will impart out of his light a form of light glorifying a renewed world. Like an avenging justice, the purifying fire encompasses the totality of the material world, the fire of purgatory, and the fire of hell. This precedes the Last Judgment. That fire, an effective power of an avenging justification, purifies and punishes spirits, souls, to the extent that they have fallen away through sin from their noble mode of being. Fire purifies them to the point where every modality not suited to the condition of renewal is dissolved.

The entire world will be renewed. It will not be totally burned up. The deformities coming from the sinful work of humanity are destroyed. Matter, that is, the four basic elements of earth, water, air, and fire (and all that exists through them), will not in its essence pass away but only in its present quality. The earth after this renewal will lose its darkness and be transparent like crystal. Fire and fiery heat will be sent to hell while luminous transparency will come to the high regions of the universe. That condition is the process of renewal. This teaching, Albert noted, fits with Christian tradition where the elements of earth, water, air, and fire lose the characteristics that have come with the conditions of contingency. Heaven with its stars will receive a greater holiness. And so the world renewed in this way will be a *new heaven* and a *new earth*. Every movement, even those in the cosmos, comes to a halt because movement – and particularly the circular movement of the spheres of heaven – serves the natural process of generation and development for beings in the realm beneath the moon. That process is complete when the number of those elected by God has been attained.

Erhard Schlieter

Albert the Great in Art

It is not so easy to bring order and sequence to the many pictures and sculptures of Albert that exist: they range from coins to large sculptures. Heribert Christian Scheeben and Angelus Walz[1] surveyed just the paintings as did Peter Dörfler.[2] Scheeben considered eighty-seven pictures while Dörfler mentioned one hundred and six artists who have created various paintings of Albert. Some works of art mentioned by Scheeben were destroyed during World War II, while new works of art picturing Albert have been created since 1945. We don't want to give here an ordered catalogue but to offer a selection of those of greater significance in the history of art and to present some works that have not yet been mentioned in articles on Albert.

Cologne is the only German city mentioned in Dante's *Divine Comedy*, and Albert is identified with Cologne in that famous poem. Albert's many years in Cologne have left traces there as has his presence in his birthplace Lauingen and in cities where he worked like Padua, Freiburg im Breisgau, Hildesheim, Regensburg, Strassburg, Paris, and Worms. Nonetheless, artistic presentations of Albert are found not only in places where Albert lived. For instance, Gerhard Marcks (1899-1981) fashioned a large bronze statue for the Cologne University in 1955, and copies of that sitting figure with the open book are found in Jena as well as at the University of Bogota, Colombia (1865) and Houston, Texas (1970) (a small bronze model for it is in the collection of the Ludwig Museum in Cologne). Albert established in Cologne a general studium of the Dominicans in the year 1248, a school now seen as the precursor of the University. As Marcks wished, Albert sits as a watcher near the main gate of the University.

There are many artistic representations of events in the life of Albertus Magnus: for instance, the work in copper by Wolfgang Kilian from 1623 at the Cologne Stadtmuseum. In Regensburg in the Albert

---

[1] *Iconographia Albertina* (Freiburg: Herder, 1932).

[2] *Albertus Magnus* (Munich: Schnell & Steiner, 1941, 1946) expanded by Hugo Schnell in 1979.

chapel on the side altar there are paintings by Joseph Altheimer and statues by Georg Schreiner. Both show scenes from the life of Albert and were done in 1896 as a gift from Albert, Prince of Thurn und Taxis.

In Cologne a window decorates the church where Albert is buried. The plan from 1952 is by Wolfram Plotzke, O.P., while the window was done in 1956: it holds eighteen scenes ranging from young Albert intrigued by nature to the death of the Dominican

Albert is depicted by some famous artists. Fra Angelico, Giovanni da Fiesole (Guido di Pietro), was born around 1400 in Vicchio and died in Rome in 1455. In the priory where he lived, San Marco in Florence, he painted between 1436 and 1445 numerous works. Among them is a famous fresco of the passion of Jesus in the chapter room of the priory. Under the fresco a frieze in the style of a predella shows many Dominicans who were important for the Order: among them is Blessed Albertus Magnus with a halo. Two further presentations are ascribed to Fra Angelico or his school: Albert in a predella of an altar in Fiesole which is now in London, and a picture of Albert as a teacher done by the school of Fra Angelico which is in Florence at the Galleria Antica e Moderna.

Before Fra Angelico, Tommaso da Modena painted Albert in 1352 on the wall of the chapter room of the St. Nicholas priory in Treviso (today a seminary). The artist depicted Albert in that room among the images of forty-two Dominicans. Tomasso da Modena (circa 1325 to 1379) belongs to the important representatives of a realism emerging in Italy in the fourteenth century. Albert wears the Dominican habit with a miter. In his room in front of him are five books. One book he has open in front of him, but his glance goes directly out of the painting to those looking at him.

Among other artists of significance is Hans Holbein the Elder (1465-1524) who completed a painting of Albert in 1501. The high altar of the former Dominican monastery in Frankfurt can be seen in the Städtisches Kunstinstitut und Museum in Frankfurt; there Albert appears in the family tree of the Dominicans set up like the tree of Jesse leading to Christ.

Joos (Justus) van Gent painted a picture of Albert around 1475 in Urbino where he was the court painter for Count Federigo di Montefeltre. He was born in Gent in 1430 and died in 1475 at Urbino, having moved to Italy in 1469. For the Count he made eighteen ideal portraits of famous philosophers and writers of antiquity and recent times. Here too is the symbol of the open book, something found frequently in pictures of Albert. There is a copy of this painting in the Dominican priory in Düsseldorf, while the original is in the Palazzo Barberini, the national museum of painting in Rome.

To remain with Urbino, no less than Luca della Robbia (1400-1482) of Florence created for the facade of the church of San Domenico in Urbino (the architect was Maso di Bartolomeo) a lunette with six figures. To the left with a lilly is St. Dominic and next to him with an open book is Thomas Aquinas. Then there is a Madonna with the Christ child; to the right Albert greets Mary and holds a book. Near him is St. Peter Martyr (at that time already the patron of the Cologne brewers).

It is also worth mentioning a painting from Amico Aspertini of Bologna (1475-1552) which shows Albert and Duns Scotus, a painting hanging in the Pinacoteca Civica in Como. There is a considerable group of presentations in copper and wood; among the more important ones are those by Tobias Stimmer (1577), Jean Jacques Boissard (1597), and Wolfgang Kilian from Augsburg (1623).

he years from 1880 to 1980 saw many presentations, most as statues. In 1981 the bank Bausparkasse Heimbau in Cologne sponsored along with the museum of the diocese of Regensburg a published guide to an exhibition of works on Albert, "Albertus Magnus, Doctor Universalis as Seen in Small Sculpture." In 1980 a new glass window was placed in St. Gereon in Cologne and in that anniversary year the Federal Republic of Germany issued a commemorative stamp.[3]

---

[3] Originally Albert was buried in the Dominican church Heilig Kreuz which was destroyed. His relics were brought in a baroque shrine with his body to the church of St. Andreas. In the nineteenth century they were in a Gothic shrine which today is in St. Andreas. Ultimately he found his last resting place in 1954 in a sarcophagus in the Roman style in the crypt of St. Andreas watched over by a bronze figure executed by Gisela Bär in 1965.

CPSIA information can be obtained
at www.ICGtesting.com
Printed in the USA
BVHW061614200120
569971BV00026B/2431

9 781623 110161